LAW, CRIME AND LAW ENF

# CRIMINAL JUSTICE IN INDIAN COUNTRY: KEY DATA

# Law, Crime and Law Enforcement

LAW, CRIME AND LAW ENFORCEMENT

# CRIMINAL JUSTICE IN INDIAN COUNTRY: KEY DATA

**Daniel Mercato**
**and**
**Elisabeth Rojas**
**EDITOR**

**Nova Science Publishers, Inc.**
*New York*

**Library of Congress Cataloging-in-Publication Data**
Criminal justice in Indian country : key data / editors, Daniel Mercato and Elisabeth Rojas.
p. cm.
Includes index.
ISBN 978-1-62100-267-3 (softcover)
1. Indians of North America--Criminal justice system. 2. Criminal justice, Administration of--United States. I. Mercato, Daniel. II. Rojas, Elisabeth. III. United States. Dept. of Justice.
E98.C87C73 2011
364.3'497073--dc23 2011031654

*Published by Nova Science Publishers, Inc. † New York*

# CONTENTS

# PREFACE

The Department of Justice has reported that the crime rates experienced by American Indians are two and a half times higher than those experienced by the general population in the United States. Specifically, from 1992 to 2001, American Indians experienced violent crimes at a rate of 101 violent crimes per 1,000 persons annually, compared to the national rate of 41 per 1,000 persons. The federal government plays a major role in prosecuting crimes committed in Indian country. For example, unless a federal statute has granted the state jurisdiction, the federal government has exclusive jurisdiction to prosecute non-Indians who commit crimes against Indians in Indian country, while the federal government and tribal governments both have jurisdiction to prosecute Indian offenders who commit crimes in Indian country. This book explores criminal justice in Native American communities with a focus on tribal crime data and an overview of their jails.

Chapter 1- The Tribal Law and Order Act (TLOA), enacted July 29, 2010, requires the Bureau of Justice Statistics (BJS) to (1) establish and implement a tribal data collection system and (2) support tribal participation in national records and information systems (P.L. 111-211, 124 Stat. 2258, § 251(b)). The act further requires the director of BJS to consult with Indian tribes to establish and implement this data collection system. The BJS director is required to report to Congress within one year of enactment, and annually thereafter, the data collected and analyzed in accordance with the act. This report describes activities in support of BJS's tribal crime data collection system and summarizes findings published from that system between July 2010 and June 2011.

Chapter 2- At midyear 2009, a total of 2,176 inmates were confined in Indian country jails, a 1.9% increase from the 2,135 inmates confined at midyear 2008 (figure 1). This count was based on data from 80 facilities, including jails, confinement facilities, detention centers, and other correctional facilities, that were in operation in Indian country at midyear 2009. For 2008, the number of inmates was based on data for 82 facilities in operation at midyear 2008. The number of inmates held in Indian country jails between 2004 and 2009 increased by 25% from 1,745 to 2,176. On June 30, 2009, the number of American Indians and Alaska Natives confined in jails outside of Indian country (9,400) was more than 4 times the number held in jails in Indian country.

Chapter 3- The Department of Justice (DOJ) has reported that the crime rates experienced by American Indians are two and a half times higher than those experienced by the general population in the United States. Specifically, from 1992 to 2001 American Indians experienced violent crimes at a rate of 101 violent crimes per 1,000 persons annually, compared to the national rate of 41 per 1,000 persons. The federal government plays a major role in prosecuting crimes committed in Indian country. For example, unless a federal statute has granted the state jurisdiction, the federal government has exclusive jurisdiction to prosecute non-Indians who commit crimes against Indians in Indian country, while the federal government and tribal governments both have jurisdiction to prosecute Indian offenders who commit crimes in Indian country. Federal prosecution, however, carries with it the possibility of greater terms of imprisonment, as tribal courts are statutorily limited to a maximum of 3 years imprisonment per offense, regardless of the severity of the offense, for example, a homicide.[1] Because of such jurisdictional and sentencing limitations, tribal communities rely on the federal government to investigate and prosecute a variety of crimes in Indian country.

In: Criminal Justice in Indian Country
Editors: D. Mercato and E. Rojas
ISBN: 978-1-62100-267-3


*Chapter 1*

# COMPENDIUM OF TRIBAL CRIME DATA, 2011*

## *United States Department of Justice*

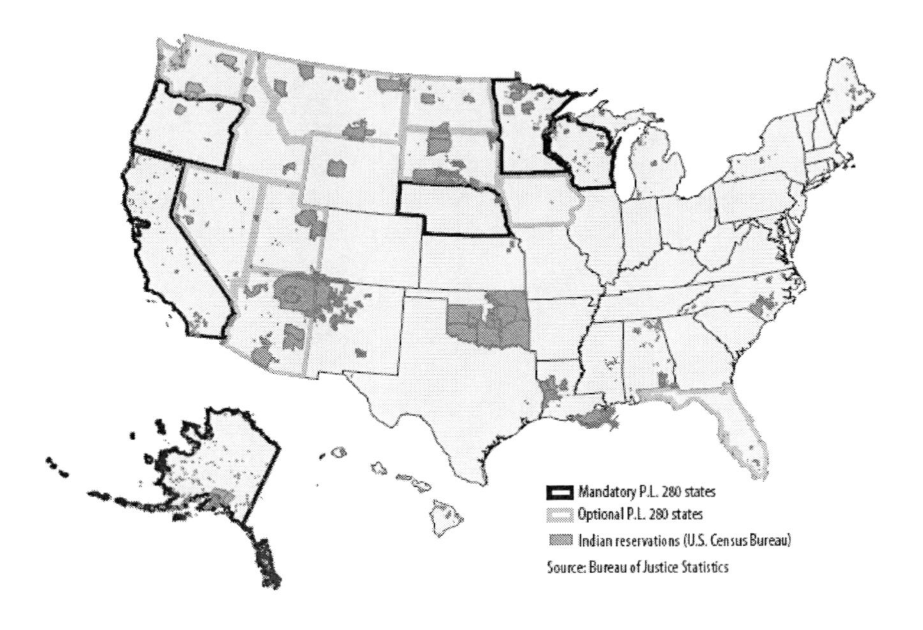


* This is an edited, reformatted and augmented version of the United States Department of Justice publication, dated June 2011.

**Bureau of Justice Statistics**
James P. Lynch
Director

**BJS Website:**
www.bjs.gov

For information contact:
BJS Clearinghouse
1-800-732-3277

The Bureau of Justice Statistics
is the statistics agency of the
U.S. Department of Justice.

Duren Banks coordinated the development of this compendium.
Contributing authors include Duren Banks, Allina Lee, Ron Malega, Todd Minton, Mark Motivans, Steven W. Perry, Brian Reaves, and Howard Snyder.

In addition to the authors, other BJS staff who contributed to verification include Paul Guerino, Tracey Kyckelhahn, and Tracy L. Snell.

Morgan Young and Jill Thomas edited the report, Barbara Quinn designed and produced the report, and Jayne Robinson and Tina Dorsey prepared the report for final printing under the supervision of Doris J. James.

June 2011, NCJ 234459

# OVERVIEW

The Tribal Law and Order Act (TLOA), enacted July 29, 2010, requires the Bureau of Justice Statistics (BJS) to (1) establish and implement a tribal data collection system and (2) support tribal participation in national records and information systems (P.L. 111-211, 124 Stat. 2258, § 251(b)). The act further requires the director of BJS to consult with Indian tribes to establish and implement this data collection system. The BJS director is required to report to Congress within one year of enactment, and annually thereafter, the data collected and analyzed in accordance with the act. This report describes activities in support of BJS's tribal crime data collection system and summarizes findings published from that system between July 2010 and June 2011.

## Multifaceted Data Collection System

Criminal jurisdiction in Indian country—federally recognized reservations, tribal communities, and identified trust lands—varies by the type of crime committed, whether the offender or victim was a tribal member, and the state in which the offense occurred. Due to the sovereign status of federally recognized tribes in the United States, crimes committed in Indian country are often subject to concurrent jurisdiction between multiple criminal justice agencies.

Public Law 83-280 (P.L. 280) gave select states legal jurisdiction over tribal members to prosecute crimes that occur on the reservation under existing state laws. These mandatory P.L. 280 states include California, Minnesota (except the Red Lake Reservation), Nebraska, Oregon (except the Warm Springs Reservation), Wisconsin, and Alaska.

P.L. 280 permitted other states to acquire jurisdiction over crimes committed in Indian country at their option. These optional P.L. 280 states assume jurisdiction, either in whole or in part, over Indian country within their boundaries, and include Arizona, Florida, Idaho, Iowa, Montana, Nevada, North Dakota, South Dakota, Utah, and Washington.

In the remaining states, where P.L. 280 does not apply, federal and tribal governments maintain concurrent jurisdiction for major crimes committed in Indian country (as defined in the Major Crimes Act and subsequent amendments (18 U.S.C. § 1153)). Tribal governments have jurisdiction for all other crimes committed in Indian country that involve both an Indian offender and Indian victim. States retain jurisdiction for non-Indian crimes committed in Indian country—those in which neither the offender nor the victim is a tribal member.

Due in part to these jurisdictional complexities, existing tribal data systems are often limited in scope and applicable only to certain jurisdictions or states. An effective tribal data collection system will include data from federal, state, local, and tribal agencies. The information maintained in this system should further be considered in light of the concurrent jurisdictional roles multiple agencies maintain in Indian country.

## Recent Findings from the Tribal Data Collection System

***178 Tribal Law Enforcement Agencies Operated in 2008***

In September 2008, American Indian tribes operated 178 law enforcement agencies. These 178 agencies employed at least one full-time sworn officer with general arrest powers or the equivalent in part-time officers. The total includes 157 general purpose tribal police departments and 21 special jurisdiction agencies tasked with enforcing natural resources laws that pertain primarily to hunting and fishing on tribal lands.

Tribes operated law enforcement agencies in 28 states and employed about 3,000 full-time sworn personnel. Eleven of the 25 largest tribal law enforcement agencies served jurisdictions of more than 1,000 square miles. (See *Tribal Law Enforcement, 2008,* for more information.)

***83 Tribal Law Enforcement Agencies Provided Data through the Bureau of Indian Affairs (BIA) that Met the FBI's Guidelines for Publication***

Offenses known to tribal law enforcement agencies were reported by tribal agencies in the FBI's *Crime in the United States, 2009*. Eighty-three tribal law enforcement agencies met FBI guidelines for data publication in the report.[1] Nearly 3,800 violent crimes and approximately 11,400 property crimes were known to these selected tribal law enforcement agencies in 2009. (See the FBI's *Crime in the United States, 2009,* http:// www2.fbi.gov/ucr/cius2009/ data/ table_11.html, for more information.)

***93 State Prosecutors' Offices in P.L. 280 States Reported Jurisdiction for Felonies Committed in Indian Country***

In 2007, 93 state court prosecutors' offices reported jurisdiction under P.L. 280 for felonies committed in Indian country. Seventy-three percent of these offices reported prosecuting at least one felony case that arose from Indian country in 2007, including at least one offense that involved drugs (63%), domestic violence (60%), or aggravated assault (58%). Most state prosecutors' offices with jurisdiction under P.L. 280 served districts with 100,000 or fewer residents. (See *State Prosecutors' Offices with Jurisdiction in Indian Country, 2007,* for more information.)

---

[1] Crimes known to tribal law enforcement agencies are submitted to the UCR through the BIA. UCR data must be submitted by local law enforcement with a valid reporting number, and be complete for all 12 months of the year. Data submitted to the UCR must also meet FBI data quality guidelines for publication in Crime in the U.S.

***Jails in Indian Country Housed 2,176 Inmates in 2009***

The number of inmates confined in Indian country jails increased by 1.9% between midyear 2008 and midyear 2009, from 2,135 to 2,176 inmates. Over the 12 months ending June 2009, the average daily jail population in Indian country increased by 12%, and the percentage of occupied bed space increased from 64.2% to 73.5%. (See *Selected Findings: Jails in Indian Country, 2009*, for more information.)

***Most Tribal Youth in the Federal System Were Referred for Violent Offenses***

Between 1999 and 2008, 65% of tribal youth in criminal matters received by federal prosecutors were referred for a violent offense. Sexual abuse was the most common violent offense, followed by assault and murder.

In 2008, federal prosecutors received 129 tribal youth suspects in matters opened out of 178,570 total matters investigated. Tribal youth admitted to the legal custody of federal prison authorities were mostly male (90%) and tended to be older teens; more than two-thirds were between the ages 16 and 17. (See Summary: *Tribal Youth in the Federal Justice System,* for more in-formation.)

## TRIBAL CRIME DATA COLLECTION ACTIVITIES, 2011

Duren Banks, Ph.D., and Steven W. Perry,
*BJS Statisticians* Allina Lee, *BJS Policy Analyst*

The Bureau of Justice Statistics (BJS), in collaboration with other federal agencies and American Indian tribes, conducted several activities to develop the tribal data collection system as of June 2011. The data collection system establishes both new data collections and enhances current programs to carry out the requirements of the Tribal Law and Order Act (TLOA), 2010.

BJS focused on improving tribal law enforcement reporting to the FBI's Uniform Crime Reporting Program (UCR) and developed direct data collection from tribal criminal justice systems, such as collecting information about the nature and operation of tribal court systems. Efforts also include activities and funding opportunities to improve tribal crime data collection through programs such as the National Criminal History Improvement Program (NCHIP), the National Instant Criminal Background Check System (NICS), Byrne/JAG funding, and UCR training.

## Activities to Support Tribal Crime Data Collection Systems, July 2010 through June 2011

***Tribal Consultations Conducted in 2010***

BJS consulted with tribal leaders through a variety of forums in 2010. BJS developed and distributed an initial plan that responded to the TLOA sections that directly referenced tribal crime data collection. This plan was presented to several stakeholder groups to invite feedback and input, including—

- Interdepartmental Tribal Justice Safety and Wellness Consultation, Session 12 (December 2010, Palm Springs, CA)
- Uniform Crime Reporting Program (UCR) trainings for tribal law enforcement (2010) agencies
- National Congress of American Indians, 2011 Executive Council Winter Meeting (March 2011, Washington, DC).

***For the First Time, the Bureau of Indian Affairs' (BIA) Submissions to UCR Were Disaggregated by Tribe and Reported in the FBI's Crime in the U.S., 2009***

Working with the Office of Justice Services in the BIA, and the Office of Tribal Justice and the FBI in the Department of Justice (DOJ), BJS developed a process to support tribal access to, and input in, regional and national criminal justice databases, including the National Crime Information Center (NCIC) and the Uniform Crime Reporting Program (UCR).

As a result of this process, data provided to the FBI from the BIA were able to be disaggregated by tribe. Offenses known to tribal law enforcement agencies were reported by tribal agencies in the FBI's *Crime in the United States, 2009*. Eighty-three tribal law enforcement agencies met FBI guidelines for data to be published in the report.

## Highlights

- The Bureau of Justice Statistics (BJS) consulted with tribal leaders through a variety of forums in 2010.
- For the first time, the Bureau of Indian Affairs' (BIA) submissions to the Uniform Crime Reporting Program (UCR) were disaggregated by tribe and reported in *Crime in the U.S., 2009.*

- The number of tribes eligible for Byrne/JAG funding increased from 5 in 2008 to 22 in 2010.
- In 2010, 140 tribal law enforcement staff received UCR training.
- BJS provided competitive funding opportunities for jurisdictions to improve criminal records in fiscal year 2011.
- BJS developed a multifaceted data collection system that both established new collections and enhanced current programs.

| BJS, acting jointly with the Office of Justice Services, BIA (DOI), and the FBI (DOJ), will work with tribes and tribal law enforcement to establish and implement tribal data collection systems (P.L. 111-211 § 251(b)). |
| --- |

***The Number of Tribes Eligible for Byrne/ JAG Funding Increased from 5 in Fiscal Year 2008 to 22 in Fiscal Year 2010***

Collaborative efforts between the departments of Justice and Interior have increased the number of tribes reporting monthly crime data to the UCR, thereby increasing the number of tribes eligible to receive Byrne/JAG awards.

Byrne/JAG funds can be used to support a range of activities in seven broad program areas, including law enforcement; prosecution and courts; crime prevention and education; corrections; drug treatment and enforcement; program planning, evaluation, and technology improvement; and crime victim and witness programs.

Most American Indian tribes had been ineligible to receive Byrne/JAG funds because of gaps in Indian country crime statistics and traditional methods for reporting data. Prior to 2009, BIA provided an aggregate number of crimes known to tribal law enforcement to the UCR. Since these data could not be disaggregated by tribe, tribal law enforcement agencies that did not submit information directly to the UCR were not eligible for Byrne/JAG awards. In FY 2008, 25 tribes submitted crime data directly to the FBI, with 5 of the tribes eligible to receive Byrne/JAG awards totaling $150,000. In FY 2010, the number of tribes that submitted crime data increased to 144 following collaborative efforts between agencies in the departments of Justice and Interior, with 22 tribes eligible for Byrne/JAG awards totaling $709,000 (table 1.1).

***More than 140 Tribal Law Enforcement Staff Received UCR Training***

Through Recovery Act funds, BJS developed and implemented the Tribal Crime Data project to further support the reporting of tribal crime to the UCR, and thereby establish eligibility for Byrne/ JAG funds. The project is also part of BJS's larger effort to collect more reliable information on American Indians in the criminal justice system and crimes committed in Indian country.

Through the Tribal Crime Data project, BJS conducted three training sessions in 2010, with more than 140 tribal members, on the use of the UCR systems. In 2011 the project provided training and technical assistance to tribes that did not meet FBI data quality guidelines or had not previously submitted complete crime data to BIA.

**Table 1.1. Tribes submitting crime data to the Uniform Crime Reporting Program (UCR) and receiving Justice Assistance Grant (JAG) awards, FY 2008–2010**

| | Number of tribes— | | |
|---|---|---|---|
| Fiscal Year | Reporting to UCR | Eligible for JAG award | Eligible award amount |
| 2008 | 25 | 5 | $150,000 |
| 2009 | 106 | 20 | 559,000 |
| 2010 | 144 | 22 | 709,000 |

### *Funding for Improving Criminal Records*

To improve criminal records, BJS provided outreach to agencies in tribal jurisdictions through two competitive funding opportunities:

- National Criminal History Improvement Program (NCHIP) solicitation, 2011
- National Instant Criminal Background Check System (NICS) Act Record Improvement Program (NARIP) solicitation, 2011.

The TLOA made federally recognized tribes eligible for awards under BJS's NCHIP.

State and tribal entities apply for NCHIP funds to enhance the crime fighting and criminal justice capabilities of governments by improving the accuracy, utility, and interstate accessibility of criminal history records. Jurisdictions also apply for NCHIP funds to enhance records of protective orders that involve domestic violence and stalking, sex offender records, automated identification systems, and other state systems that support national records systems and their use for criminal history background checks.

BJS released the FY 2011 NCHIP solicitation on January 13, 2011, and collaborated with other OJP components to disseminate information about the NCHIP funding announcement as broadly as possible. Tribal contacts were alerted via email to the funding opportunity, and the solicitation was posted to the BJS and DOJ Tribal Safety and Justice websites. Information about the NCHIP funding opportunity was also presented during several meetings and a consultation in the fall and winter of 2010.

Additionally, BJS developed an addendum to the solicitation that identified priority funding areas and eligibility requirements for tribal applicants. The addendum outlined key tribal priority areas activities related to—

- information technology systems to capture and transmit tribal issued domestic violence and stalking records to the FBI NCIC Protection Order File
- automation and transmission of existing qualifying domestic violence and stalking records to the FBI NCIC Protection Order File.

The NARIP implements the provisions of the NICS Improvement Amendments Act of 2007, enacted in the wake of the shooting tragedy at Virginia Tech and includes tribes as eligible entities.

The NARIP funds provide assistance to eligible states and tribes to improve the completeness, automation, and transmittal of records needed by the NICS to identify persons prohibited from receiving or possessing a firearm. These records include prohibited mental health adjudications and commitments, felony convictions, felony indictments, fugitives from justice, drug arrests and convictions, domestic violence protection orders, and misdemeanor crimes of domestic violence.

> BJS is authorized to provide for improvements in the accuracy, quality, timeliness, immediate accessibility, and integration of state and tribal criminal history and related records (P.L. 111-211 § 251(b)(1)(H)).

BJS will award FY 2011 NARIP funds to support efforts to improve the records used by NICS, by providing assistance to states and tribes to improve the completeness, automation, and transmittal of records to state and federal systems. BJS released the FY 2011 NARIP solicitation on March 15, 2011.

The same process used to disseminate information about the NCHIP funding opportunity was followed to alert tribes to the NARIP solicitation.

Subject to the availability of appropriated funds and any modifications or additional requirements that may be imposed by law, BJS plans to competitively award NCHIP and NARIP funds in FY 2011. Eligible applications will be evaluated and scored by peer reviewers, and funding will be made based on the selection criteria outlined in the solicitations.

> The director of BJS will establish and implement a tribal data collection system (P.L. 111-211 § 251(b)).

## BJS Established New Collections and Enhanced Current Programs

In addition to collaborating with other federal agencies to improve tribal law enforcement reporting to the UCR, BJS developed a plan to collect information about tribal criminal justice systems. This multipronged approach both established new collections and enhanced current programs that serve the purposes of the TLOA.

Through its ongoing statistical projects, BJS provided information on (1) suspects and defendants processed in the federal criminal justice system, including federal prosecutions of crimes committed in Indian country, (2) the incidence of crimes known to law enforcement that occur on tribal reservations or were reported by Indian country law enforcement authorities, (3) the characteristics of tribal law enforcement agencies, and (4) the characteristics of jails in Indian country. BJS plans to begin collecting information about the nature and operation of tribal court systems in 2012 (table 1.2).

### *Survey of Tribal Court Systems*

BJS developed the Survey of Tribal Court Systems to build on BJS's previous Census of Tribal Justice Agencies (See *Census of Tribal Justice Agencies in Indian Country, 2002,* BJS Web, December 2005). The survey will gather administrative and operational information from tribal courts, prosecutors' offices, and indigent defense providers operating in the estimated 190 federally recognized tribal justice systems in the U.S. Subject to the availability of appropriated funds and any modifications or additional requirements that may be imposed by law, BJS plans to award the Survey of Tribal Court Systems in FY 2011. BJS will work with the awardee and collaborating organizations to develop the data collection instrument and methodology. The instrument will include, at a minimum, measures of tribal court organization, court caseload, characteristics of prosecutors in tribal courts, and systems to provide indigent defense in tribal courts.

Based on the results of the initial data collection, BJS will devise a strategy for conducting a regular data collection program among Indian country court systems.

***Census of State and Local Law Enforcement Agencies***

The Census of State and Local Law Enforcement Agencies provides data on staffing, functions, and expenditures. Data collected include the number of sworn and civilian personnel by state and type of agency, and functions performed by each agency. BJS analyzed and published findings from data collected in 2008, from the Census of State and Local Law Enforcement Agencies program, including 178 tribal law enforcement agencies.

***Survey of Jails in Indian Country***

The Survey of Jails in Indian Country data describe jails, confinement facilities, detention centers, and other facilities operated by tribal authorities or BIA. The annual report from the Survey of Jails in Indian Country includes data on the number of adults and juveniles held, type of offense, number of persons confined on the last weekday of each month, average daily population, peak population, and admissions at midyear. It also summarizes rated capacity, facility crowding, and jail staffing. The most recent report that describes findings from the 2009 survey was released in February 2011.

***National Census of State Court Prosecutors***

In 2007 BJS conducted the National Census of State Prosecutors, which was the second complete enumeration of all chief prosecutors who tried felony cases in state courts of general jurisdiction. The census collected information about whether district attorney offices have jurisdiction for prosecuting felony cases occurring in Indian country under P.L. 280, and what types of crimes the office prosecuted. The findings from this data collection are in *State Prosecutors' Offices with Jurisdiction in Indian Country*

## Table 1.2. Bureau of Justice Statistics Planned Program Activities in Response to the Tribal Law and Order Act

| Program | Objective | Timeline |
|---|---|---|
| Collaboration with DOJ Components and BIA | To increase the number of tribes eligible to receive Edward Byrne Memorial Justice Assistance Grant (JAG) Program funds, ensure tribal access to regional and national databases, and develop comprehensive tribal crime data systems. | Ongoing. |
| BJS Recovery Act Program | To support tribes to more accurately and consistently report tribal crime data to the BIA and/or the FBI through technical assistance, training, and information sharing. | Crimes known to some tribal law enforcement agencies published in Crime in the United States, 2009 and annually thereafter. |
| Grants to Support Tribal Participation in Regional and National Databases | To continue to include federally-recognized tribes as eligible entities for the National Instant Criminal Background Check System (NICS) Act Record Improvement Program and add federally-recognized tribes as eligible entities to the National Criminal History Improvement Program (NCHIP) grant awards. | Tribes are eligible for awards as of FY 2009 (NICS) and FY 2011 (NCHIP). |
| Census of State and Local Law Enforcement Agencies | To collect data from all state, local, and tribal law enforcement agencies on staffing, expenditures and functions. BJS will continue to implement strategies designed to accurately represent the work of tribal law enforcement agencies. | Periodically since 1992. Latest report: 2004 census 2008 census report in 2011. |
| Survey of Tribal Court Systems | To gather administrative and operational information from tribal courts, prosecutors' offices, and indigent defense providers. | Award: August 2011. Design and Data Collection: 2011-2012. Analysis and Reporting: Early 2013. |
| Survey of Jails in Indian Country | The survey is an annual enumeration of jails, confinement facilities, detention centers, and other facilities operated by tribal authorities or the BIA. | Annually since 1998. Latest report: 2009 survey 2010 survey report expected in 2011. |

| Program | Objective | Timeline |
|---|---|---|
| | Data are collected intermittently via an addendum to the core survey on the physical conditions and operations of Indian country facilities. The addendum requests information on inmate medical services, mental health services, suicide prevention procedures, substance dependency programs, domestic violence counseling, sex offender treatment, education programs, and inmate work assignments. | |
| Federal Justice Statistics Program | To compile comprehensive information describing suspects and defendants processed in the federal criminal justice system. | Ongoing since 1998. Annual data through 2009 available on the BJS website. |
| BJS Native American Crime Information Website | To provide users with easy-to-access and current information from existing and new data collection programs | Design and populate website: 2010-2011. Public release: Late 2011. |

### ***Federal Justice Statistics Program***

The Federal Justice Statistics Program (FJSP) provides comprehensive and detailed information about the federal justice system's processing of criminal cases. The FJSP provides annual data on workload, activities, and outcomes associated with federal criminal cases. Information is acquired on all aspects of processing in the federal justice system, including arrests, prosecution decisions, referrals to magistrates, court dispositions, sentencing outcomes, sentence length, and time served. The FJSP receives the source data from the U.S. Marshals Service, Drug Enforcement Administration, Executive Office of U.S. Attorneys, Administrative Office of the U.S. Courts, U.S. Sentencing Commission, and the Federal Bureau of Prisons.

BJS is currently developing research projects that will examine American Indian defendants who are processed in the federal justice system. Findings from the first of these projects, describing characteristics of American Indian youth who are processed in the federal criminal justice system, are in the *Summary: Tribal Youth in the Federal Justice System*.

## References

*Crime in the United States, 2009*, U.S. Department of Justice, Federal Bureau of Investigation, September 2010.

*Jails in Indian Country, 2009,* NCJ 232223, BJS Web, February 2011.

*State Prosecutors Offices with Jurisdiction in Indian Country, 2007,* NCJ 234241, BJS Web, June 2011.

*Tribal Law Enforcement, 2008.* NCJ 234217, BJS Web, June 2011.

*Summary: Tribal Youth in the Federal Justice System,* NCJ 234218, BJS Web, June 2011.

# TRIBAL LAW ENFORCEMENT, 2008

Brian A. Reaves, Ph.D., *BJS Statistician*

In September 2008, American Indian tribes operated 178 law enforcement agencies that employed at least one full-time sworn officer with general arrest powers or the equivalent in part-time officers. The total includes 157 general purpose tribal police departments and 21 special jurisdiction agencies tasked with enforcing natural resources laws that pertain primarily to hunting and fishing on tribal lands.

Collectively, tribes operated law enforcement agencies in 28 states. Washington (24), Arizona (22), Oklahoma (19), and New Mexico (17) had the largest numbers of tribal law enforcement agencies (figure 2.1). These findings are based on the 2008 Bureau of Justice Statistics' (BJS) Census of State and Local Law Enforcement Agencies.

In addition to tribally operated agencies, the Department of the Interior's (DOI) Bureau of Indian Affairs (BIA) operated 42 agencies that provided law enforcement services in Indian country. Nationwide, BIA employed 277 full-time sworn personnel in 2008. Along with direct oversight of its own programs, BIA also provided technical assistance and some oversight to tribally operated agencies.

On the more than 300 federal Indian reservation areas in the U.S., police officers may be tribal, federal, state, county, or municipal employees. Some areas may be served by more than one type of officer.

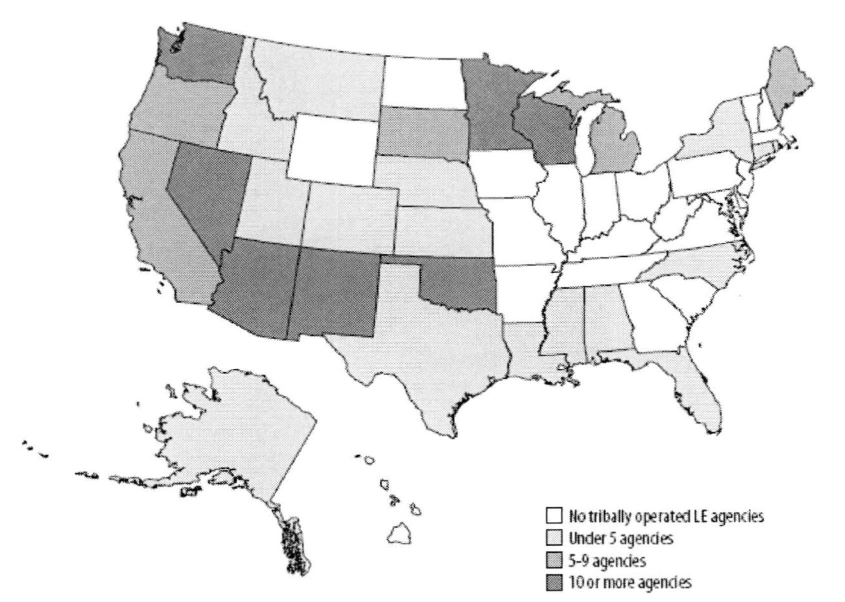


Source: Bureau of Justice Statistics, Census of State and Local Law Enforcement Agencies, 2008.

Figure 2.1. Location of tribally operated law enforcement agencies, 2008.

## Highlights

- Tribally operated law enforcement agencies employed nearly 4,600 full-time personnel, including about 3,000 sworn officers.
- The largest tribal law enforcement agency, the Navajo Police Department, employed 393 full-time sworn personnel in Arizona, New Mexico, and Utah.
- Eleven of the 25 largest tribal law enforcement agencies served jurisdictions covering more than 1,000 square miles.
- Overall, tribal police departments cost about $257 per resident to operate during FY 2008.
- In addition to law enforcement functions, nearly all tribal police departments performed court-related functions, such as court security and serving process.
- More than half of tribal police departments used community policing officers, and more than a third used school resource officers.
- About 4 in 5 tribal police departments participated in one or more multiagency task forces.

Commonly, tribal police department funding, administration, and employees are based on the Indian Self-Determination and Education Assistance Act of 1975, (Public Law 93-638 or P.L. 638). This law allowed tribes to assume responsibility for many programs previously administered by the federal government, including law enforcement. P.L. 638 agencies operate with tribal employees under contract and with financial assistance from the BIA.

Tribally operated agencies can also function under a self-governance compact with the BIA. This arrangement provides block grant payments, allowing for more tribal control than the line item funding of P.L. 638 contracts. Full tribal control over law enforcement services exists where such services are entirely funded by the tribal government.

Jurisdiction over offenses in Indian country may lie with federal, state, or tribal agencies, depending on the offense, offender, victim, and offense location. Most tribes have crossdeputization agreements, often with neighboring nontribal agencies. These agreements allow law enforcement personnel from state, local, and tribal entities to cross jurisdictions in criminal cases, and can be used to enhance law enforcement capabilities in areas where state and tribal lands are contiguous and intermingled. In some instances, the number of agreements is large. For example, the Cherokee Nation Marshal Service is cross-deputized with 50 municipal, county, state, and federal agencies.

### *Tribal Police Departments Employed 2.3 Full-Time Officers Per 1,000 Residents*

In September 2008, the 178 operating tribal law enforcement agencies employed more than 4,500 full-time personnel, including about 3,000 sworn officers (table 2.1). The 157 general purpose tribal police departments employed 4,294 full-time personnel, including 2,835 sworn officers and 1,459 civilian personnel. These agencies employed an additional 129 part-time personnel, including 80 sworn officers (not shown in table).

The 21 natural resources agencies employed 271 full-time personnel, including 164 sworn officers and 107 civilian employees. These natural resources agencies also employed 11 part-time personnel, including 7 sworn officers (not shown in table).

## Table 2.1. Tribally operated law enforcement agencies, by type of agency and number of full-time sworn personnel, 2008

| Type of agency and number of full-time sworn personnel | Number of agencies | Number of full-time employees Total Sworn Civilian | | |
|---|---|---|---|---|
| All agencies | 178 | 4,565 | 2,999 | 1,566 |
| General purpose police departments | | | | |
| Total | 157 | 4,294 | 2,835 | 1,459 |
| 50 or more | 6 | 1,397 | 871 | 526 |
| 25-49 | 19 | 955 | 607 | 348 |
| 10-24 | 61 | 1,380 | 955 | 425 |
| 5-9 | 47 | 479 | 332 | 147 |
| Under 5 | 24 | 83 | 70 | 13 |
| Natural resources agencies | | | | |
| Total | 21 | 271 | 164 | 107 |
| 10-24 | 8 | 154 | 107 | 47 |
| 5-9 | 4 | 38 | 29 | 9 |
| Under 5 | 9 | 79 | 28 | 51 |

General purpose tribal police departments had a combined service population of about 1.2 million residents.[2] This corresponds to about 2.3 full-time sworn officers per 1,000 residents, which was the national average for all local police departments as of 2007. (See *Local Police Departments, 2007,* BJS Web, December 2010.) Collectively, tribal police departments cost $257 per resident to operate for 2008 (not shown in table). In 2007 the national average for all local police departments was $260 per resident.

### *11 of the 25 Largest Tribal Law Enforcement Agencies Served Jurisdictions of More than 1,000 Square Miles*

The 25 largest tribally operated agencies employed at least 25 full-time sworn personnel. The largest agency, the Navajo Police Department, employed 393 full-time officers to serve tribal lands in Arizona, New Mexico, and Utah (table 2.2). The next largest were the Seminole Police Department (Florida) with 144 officers, and the Salt River Police Department (Arizona) with 125 officers.

The BIA service population for the 25 largest agencies ranged from less than 1,000 to about 200,000 residents. Although not all reservations are open to the public, many tribal law enforcement agencies deal with a significant number of daily visitors in addition to the resident population. The natural resources of tribal lands attract visitors, as do conference facilities and casinos. All of the 25 largest agencies had at least one casino operating within their jurisdictional area.

The amount of land area served by a tribal law enforcement agency can be quite large. For example, the Navajo Police Department has jurisdiction over about 22,000 square miles, a larger land area than any county in the continental United States. Ten other agencies among the 25 largest had jurisdictional areas exceeding 1,000 square miles, a larger land area than any city in the continental United States.

---

[2] Based on the American Indian service population counts published in BIA's American Indian Population and Labor Force Report, 2005. The service population is the total number of enrolled tribal members and members from other tribes who live on or near the reservation and are eligible to use the BIAfunded tribal services. The service population excludes any non-Indian residents served by a tribally operated law enforcement agency and other persons using roads, stores, casinos, and other public places on tribal land.

**Table 2.2. The 25 largest tribally operated law enforcement agencies, by the number of full-time sworn personnel, 2008**

| Name and location of agency | Number of full-time sworn personnel | BIA service population, 2005 | Full-time sworn personnel per 1,000 residents | Reservation land area (square miles) | Full-time sworn personnel per 25 square miles |
|---|---|---|---|---|---|
| Navajo Police Department (AZ, NM, UT) | 393 | 192,067 | 2.0 | 22,174 | 0.4 |
| Seminole Police Department (FL) | 144 | 3,165 | 45.5 | 141 | 25.5 |
| Salt River Police Department (AZ) | 125 | 7,313 | 17.1 | 81 | 38.6 |
| Gila River Indian Community Police | 93 | 14,966 | 6.2 | 584 | 4.0 |
| Tohono O'odham Police Department (AZ) | 66 | 26,673 | 2.5 | 4,453 | 0.4 |
| Choctaw Police Department (MS) | 50 | 8,313 | 6.0 | 25 | 50.0 |
| Oglala Sioux Tribe Department of Public Safety (SD) | 49 | 43,146 | 1.1 | 3,159 | 0.4 |
| Cherokee Indian Police Department (NC) | 45 | 13,562 | 3.3 | 83 | 13.6 |
| Muscogee (Creek) Nation Lighthorse Tribal Police (OK) | 39 | 55,817 | 0.7 | 4,648 | 0.2 |
| Miccosukee Police Department (FL) | 36 | 589 | 61.1 | 128 | 7.0 |
| Poarch Creek Tribal Police Department (AL) | 33 | 1,567 | 21.1 | 0.4 | -- |
| Cherokee Nation Marshal Service (OK) | 32 | 197,684 | 0.2 | 6,702 | 0.1 |
| Choctaw Nation Tribal Police Department | 32 | 99,371 | 0.3 | 10,613 | 0.1 |

Table 2.2. (Continued)

| Name and location of agency | Number of full-time sworn personnel | BIA service population, 2005 | Full-time sworn personnel per 1,000 residents | Reservation land area (square miles) | Full-time sworn personnel per 25 square miles |
|---|---|---|---|---|---|
| Colville Tribal Police Department (WA) | 32 | 5,052 | 6.3 | 2,117 | 0.4 |
| Saginaw Chippewa Tribal Police Department (MI) | 30 | 1,799 | 16.7 | 218 | 3.4 |
| Tulalip Tribal Police Services (WA) | 30 | 2,869 | 10.5 | 35 | 21.4 |
| Warm Springs Tribal Police Department (OR) | 30 | 4,079 | 7.4 | 1,011 | 0.7 |
| White Mountain Apache Police Department (AZ) | 30 | 12,213 | 2.5 | 2,628 | 0.3 |
| Isleta Police Department (NM) | 29 | 3,980 | 7.3 | 331 | 2.2 |
| Yakama Nation Tribal Police Department (WA) | 28 | 16,815 | 1.7 | 2,153 | 0.3 |
| Pascua Yaqui Tribal Police Department (AZ) | 27 | 14,787 | 1.8 | 2 | -- |
| Puyallup Tribal Police Department (WA) | 27 | 24,016 | 1.1 | 29 | 23.3 |
| Rosebud Sioux Tribal Police Department (SD) | 27 | 22,293 | 1.2 | 1,388 | 0.5 |
| Red Lake Tribal Police Department (MN) | 26 | 10,338 | 2.5 | 880 | 0.7 |
| Oneida Indian Nation Police (NY) | 25 | 650 | 38.5 | 0.1 | -- |

Note: Land area data are from the U.S. Census Bureau, and include reservation land only.

--Reservation land area is less than 25 square miles.

### *Tribal Law Enforcement Agencies Were Responsible for a Broad Range of Services and Functions During 2008*

Nearly all general purpose tribal police departments were responsible for traditional law enforcement functions, such as routine patrol (100%), responding to citizen requests for service (100%), special events and crowd control (98%), criminal investigation (96%), and traffic enforcement (96%) (figure 2.2). About 4 in 5 departments were responsible for parking enforcement (80%), and about 2 in 3 departments dispatched calls for service (66%).

### *About 3 in 5 General Purpose Tribal Police Departments Had Full-Time Community Policing Officers*

A majority of tribal police departments used a community policing approach in their efforts to prevent crime and maintain partnerships with the communities they serve. About three-fifths (59%) of departments had full-time sworn personnel serving as community policing officers (table 2.3). As of September 2008, about 500 tribal police officers were designated as community policing officers. In 2000, 73% of tribal agencies reported using community policing officers, with about 700 designated as such.

**Table 2.3. Use of community policing and school resource officers by tribal police departments, 2000 and 2008**

| | 2000 | 2008 |
|---|---|---|
| Community policing officers | | |
| Percent of agencies using | 73% | 59% |
| Number of officers | 714 | 503 |
| School resource officers | | |
| Percent of agencies using | 37% | 36% |
| Number of officers | 162 | 82 |

For more than a third (36%) of tribal police departments, community policing efforts extended into the schools, with 82 full-time sworn personnel assigned as school resource officers. Although the percentage of departments using school resource officers in 2008 was about the same as in 2000 (37%), the total number of officers was about half of 2000 levels.

***Nearly All Tribal Police Departments Performed a Variety of Court-Related Functions***

In addition to law enforcement duties, nearly all tribal police departments were responsible for a variety of court-related functions (figure 2.3). The most common functions were executing arrest warrants (95%), enforcing protection orders (92%), serving process (89%), apprehending fugitives (88%), and providing court security (75%).

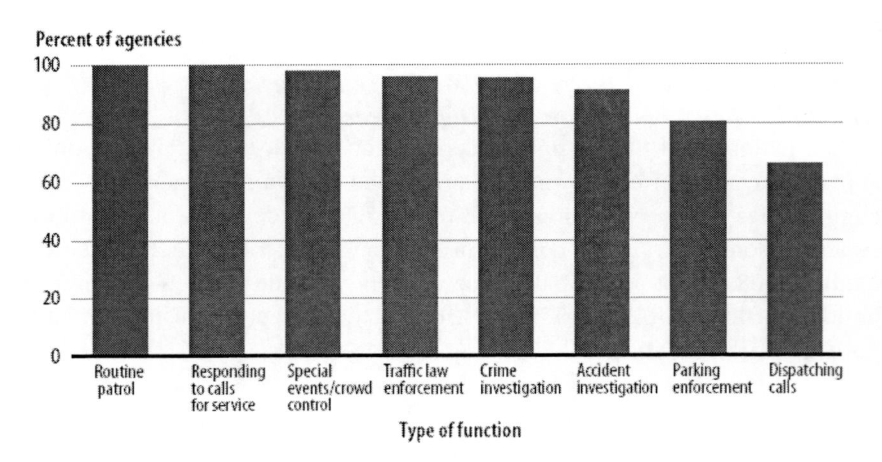


Figure 2.2. Selected law enforcement functions performed by tribal police departments, 2008.

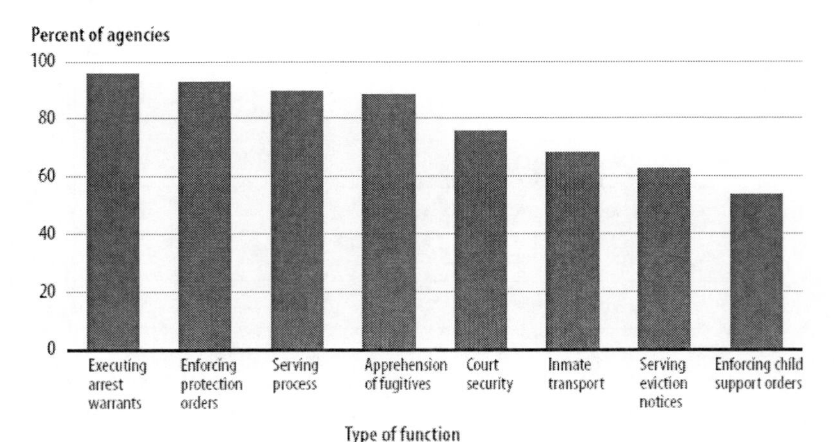


Figure 2.3. Selected court-related functions performed by tribal police departments, 2008.

### *Nearly Half of Tribal Police Departments Were Responsible for Search and Rescue Operations*

Nearly 9 in 10 tribal police departments performed one or more special public safety functions, the most common being emergency management (65%) and animal control (64%) (figure 2.4). About a third (31%) provided emergency medical services. Nearly a fifth provided fire services (19%) and school crossing services (18%).

More than half (58%) of tribal police departments performed at least one specialized function, such as search and rescue (43%), tactical operations (26%), or underwater recovery (10%). About 1 in 6 agencies operated at least one jail (17%), and about 1 in 10 agencies operated an overnight lockup fcility separate from a jail (10%). (For more information, see *Jails in Indian County, 2009*, BJS Web, February 2011.)

The 21 special jurisdiction agencies, whose primary focus was the enforcement of natural resources laws, performed a variety of functions as well. In addition to providing patrol and response services, a majority of these agencies performed the following functions: criminal investigation (82%), search and rescue (71%), apprehension of fugitives (59%), animal control (59%), traffic enforcement (59%), and dispatching calls for service (53%) (not shown in figure).

## About Two-Thirds of General Purpose Tribal Police Departments Participated in a Multiagency Drug Task Force

About 4 in 5 (78%) tribal police departments partnered with federal, state, and local agencies in multiagency task forces to combat crime problems in Indian country during 2008. These task forces allow participating agencies to share in pooled resources, information, and expertise across jurisdictional boundaries.

Tribal police departments were most likely to participate in task forces formed to combat drug trafficking (66% of agencies) (figure 2.5). About 2 in 5 (41%) departments participated in multiagency gang task forces, and about a third (32%) participated in violent crime task forces. Smaller percentages of tribal police departments participated in antiterrorism (17%) or human trafficking (9%) task forces.

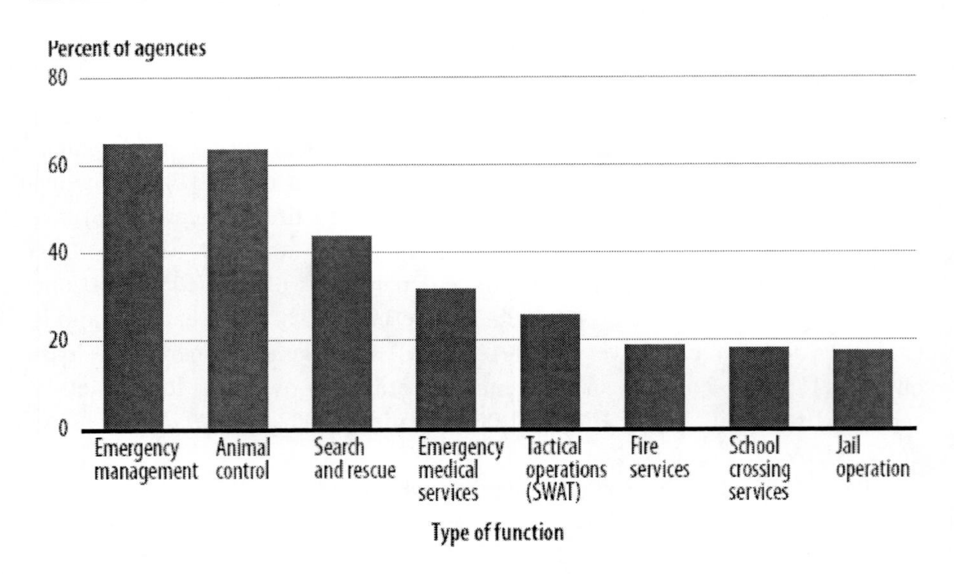


Figure 2.4. Selected special functions performed by tribal police departments, 2008.

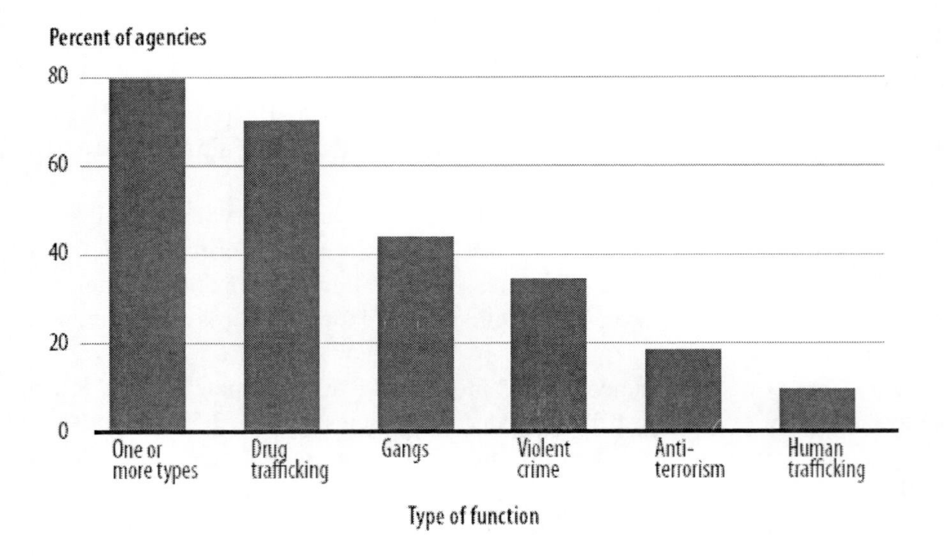


Figure 2.5. Task force participation of tribal police departments, 2008.

# METHODOLOGY

The Bureau of Justice Statistics' (BJS) Census of State and Local Law Enforcement Agencies (CSLLEA) is conducted every 4 years to provide a complete enumeration of agencies and their employees. Employment data are reported for sworn and nonsworn personnel and, within these categories, by full-time or part-time status. Agencies also complete a checklist of functions they regularly perform, or for which they have primary responsibility.

The CSLLEA provides national data on the number of state and local law enforcement agencies and employees for general purpose local police departments (including tribal agencies), sheriffs' offices, the primary state law enforcement agencies, and special jurisdiction (e.g., natural resources) agencies. It also serves as the sampling frame for BJS surveys of law enforcement agencies.

The 2008 CSLLEA form was mailed to approximately 20,000 agencies that were determined to potentially be operating on the reference date of September 30, 2008. This master list was created by compiling information from the following sources:

- the 2004 CSLLEA
- lists provided by Peace Officer Standards and Training offices, and other state agencies
- an FBI list of agencies requesting new identifiers since the 2004 CSLLEA.

Responding agencies were screened for eligibility and were excluded if any of the following conditions existed on the CSLLEA reference date of September 30, 2008:

- The agency employed only part-time officers, and the total combined hours worked for these officers averaged less than 35 hours per week.
- The agency contracted or outsourced to another agency for performance of all services.
- The agency was closed, a duplicate listing, or otherwise an invalid entry on the master list.
- The agency did not employ personnel with general arrest powers.
- The agency did not operate with funds from a state, local, special district, or tribal government.
- All sworn officers volunteered their time on an unpaid basis.

Data on number and type of personnel were obtained from all eligible tribal agencies. For general purpose tribal police departments, the item response rates were as follows: community policing and school resource officers, 100%; agency functions, 99%; task force participation, 99%; and operating budget, 87%.

## References

*American Indians and Crime,* NCJ 173386, BJS Web, February 1999.
*American Indian Population and Labor Force Report, 2005,* U.S. Department of the Interior, Bureau of Indian Affairs, Office of Indian Services.
*Census of State and Local Law Enforcement Agencies, 2008,* NCJ 233982, BJS Web, June 2011.
*Census of Tribal Justice Agencies in Indian Country, 2002,* NCJ 205332, BJS Web, December 2005.
*Indian Country Law Enforcement Review,* U.S. Department of Justice, December 1999.
*Jails in Indian Country, 2009,* NCJ 232223, BJS Web, February 2011.
*Local Police Departments, 2007,* NCJ 231174, BJS Web, December 2010.
*Policing on American Indian Reservations,* U.S. Department of Justice, National Institute of Justice, NCJ 186185, September 2001.
*Tribal Law Enforcement, 2000,* NCJ 197936, BJS Web, January 2003.

# State Prosecutors' Offices with Jurisdiction in Indian Country, 2007

Steven W. Perry, Ron Malega, Ph.D., and Duren Banks, Ph.D.,
*BJS Statisticians*

In 2007, 93 state court prosecutors' offices reported jurisdiction under Public Law 83-280 (P.L. 280) for felonies committed in Indian country. Seventy-three percent of these offices prosecuted at least one felony case that arose from Indian country in 2007, including at least one offense that involved drugs (63%), domestic violence (60%), or aggravated assault (58%).

This report presents selected findings from the Bureau of Justice Statistics's (BJS) 2007 National Census of State Prosecutors. Criminal jurisdiction in Indian country is divided among federal, state, and tribal governments. Jurisdiction in a specific incident depends on the nature of the offense, whether the offender or victim was a tribal member, and the state in which the crime occurred.

Crimes committed in Indian country are often subject to concurrent jurisdiction between multiple criminal justice agencies. The Major Crimes Act (18 U.S.C. § 1153), as amended, grants concurrent federal jurisdiction for 16 major crimes committed by Native Americans occurring in Indian country. State jurisdiction for crimes committed in Indian country is primarily provided for under P.L. 280. Tribal courts maintain concurrent jurisdiction when federal or state jurisdiction is applied.

State prosecutors' offices generally do not have jurisdiction over crimes committed in Indian country due to the sovereign status of federally recognized tribes in the United States. However, state prosecutors' offices in 16 states may exercise jurisdiction over crimes committed on tribal lands under P.L. 280. This law established state jurisdiction over offenses committed by or against American Indians in Indian country, including federally recognized reservations, tribal communities, and identified trust lands. P.L. 280 is mandatory for 6 states and optional for 10 states.

Criminal jurisdiction in Indian country

Tribal jurisdiction

- Crimes committed by Native Americans in Indian country. Sentences are limited to a maximum 3-year sentence of incarceration per count and 9 years per case (124 U.S.C. 2258 § 234 (a) (b)).

Federal jurisdiction

Pursuant to the Major Crimes Act of 1885. 18 U.S.C. § 1153
and subsequent amendments

State jurisdiction

All crimes on tribal lands specified under Public Law 83-280. 18 U.S.C. § 1162
Crimes committed on tribal lands in which neither the victim
nor the offender is a tribal member.

Note: Criminal jurisdiction in Indian country depends on several factors, including the identity of the defendant, victim, type of offense, and where the crime was committed.

## Highlights

- Ninety-three state court prosecutors' offices in the 16 P.L. 280 states reported jurisdiction for felonies committed in Indian country under P.L. 280.
- Seventy-three percent of offices with jurisdiction in Indian country reported prosecuting at least one felony case committed in Indian country.
- Most offices in P.L. 280 states prosecuted at least one offense involving drugs (63%), domestic violence (60%), or aggravated assault (58%).
- Eighteen offices in mandatory P.L. 280 states with jurisdiction for Indian country prosecuted at least one rape, and 12 offices prosecuted a homicide.
- Of state prosecutors' offices that reported jurisdiction for felony cases in Indian country under P.L. 280, 70% served judicial districts with populations of less than 100,000 residents.
- Offices with jurisdiction for felony crimes committed in Indian country had an average operating budget of $5.2 million in 2007.

According to the 2002 Census of Tribal Justice Agencies, 94 of the 123 responding tribes in mandatory P.L. 280 states relied on state courts. The 2002 Census was limited to American Indian tribes in the lower 48 states, so tribes in Alaska were excluded. The Census also found that 19 of 90 reporting tribes in optional P.L. 280 states relied on state courts (table 3.1).

The federal government retains criminal jurisdiction for major crimes committed in Indian country in the remaining states where P.L. 280 does not apply. States retain jurisdiction for non-Indian crimes (those in which neither the offender nor the victim is a tribal member) committed in Indian country.[3] In 2007, 1,548 state court prosecutors' offices were in states not affected by P.L. 280 and were excluded from this report.

The 93 state prosecutors' offices reporting jurisdiction under P.L. 280 in mandatory and optional states represent 14% of all state prosecutors' offices in states affected by P.L. 280. Nearly all of these served districts that overlapped with or were adjacent to tribal lands (figure 3.1).

---

[3] Some tribes have been affected by states that have received a federal mandate to exercise jurisdiction outside of P.L. 280, e.g., through state-wide enactments, restoration acts, or land claims settlement acts (Tribal Court Clearinghouse, 2010, www.tribal institute.org/lists/jurisdiction.htm).

***Approximately a Fifth of State Prosecutors in Mandatory P.L. 280 States Reported Jurisdiction for Crimes Committed in Indian Country***

P.L. 280 gave select states legal jurisdiction over tribal members to prosecute crimes occurring on the reservation under existing state laws. These mandatory P.L. 280 states include California, Minnesota (except the Red Lake Reservation), Nebraska, Oregon (except the Warm Springs Reservation), Wisconsin, and Alaska (table 3.2).

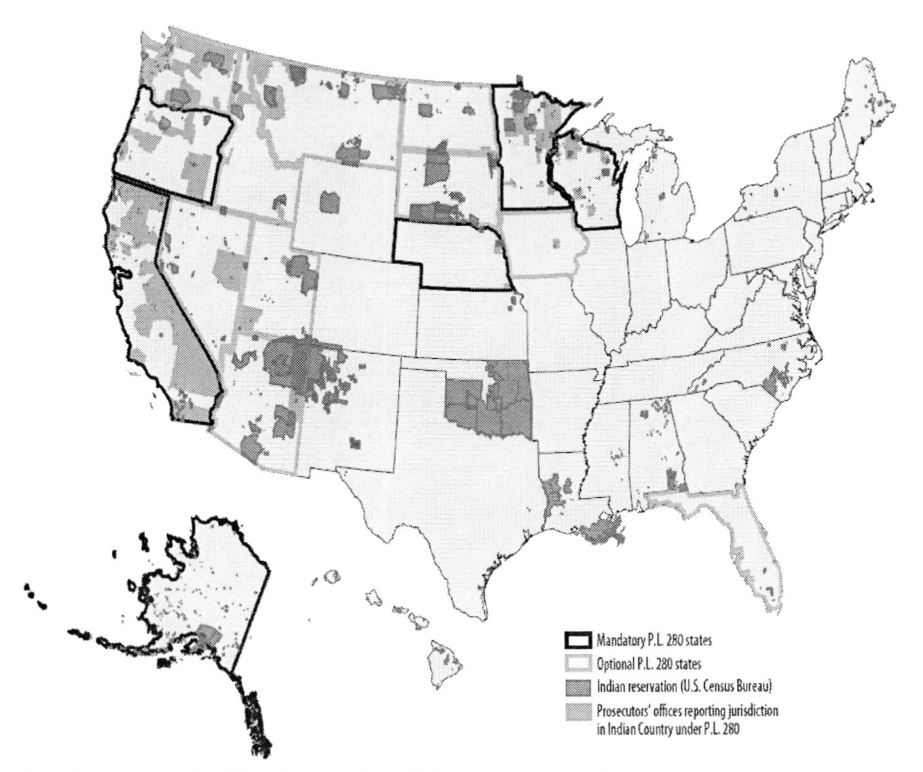


Note: Prosecutors' offices in non-P.L. 280 states are not shown.
Source: Bureau of Justice Statistics.

Figure 3.1. State prosecutors' offices reporting jurisdiction in Indian country under P.L. 280, 2007.

**Table 3.1. Number of tribes participating in the Census of Tribal Justice Agencies in Indian Country, by P.L. 280 status, type of court systems, and state, 2002**

| | | Number of tribes using— | | | | |
|---|---|---|---|---|---|---|
| | Participating in census | Tribal justice systems | Indigenous courts | CFR courts[a] | Tribal courts | Relying on state |
| Mandatory states | 123 | 39 | 8 | 9 | 37 | 94 |
| California | 88 | 7 | 2 | 7 | 7 | 74 |
| Minnesota | 12 | 12 | 3 | 0 | 12 | 4 |
| Nebraska | 4 | 3 | 0 | 2 | 3 | 2 |
| Oregon | 8 | 8 | 1 | 0 | 8 | 6 |
| Wisconsin | 11 | 9 | 2 | 0 | 7 | 8 |
| Optional states | 90 | 80 | 13 | 11 | 74 | 19 |
| Arizona | 17 | 16 | 3 | 0 | 16 | 0 |
| Florida | 1 | 0 | 0 | 0 | 0 | 1 |
| Idaho | 4 | 4 | 1 | 0 | 4 | 1 |
| Iowa | 1 | 0 | 0 | 0 | 0 | 1 |
| Montana | 6 | 6 | 1 | 0 | 5 | 0 |
| Nevada | 16 | 14 | 1 | 4 | 13 | 6 |
| North Dakota | 3 | 3 | 0 | 0 | 3 | 0 |
| South Dakota | 9 | 9 | 0 | 2 | 9 | 0 |
| Utah | 4 | 2 | 0 | 2 | 2 | 2 |
| Washington | 29 | 26 | 7 | 3 | 22 | 8 |

Note: The 2002 Census of Tribal Justice Agencies was limited to American Indian tribes in the lower 48 states. Source: Table reproduced from *Census of Tribal Justice Agencies in Indian Country, 2002*, NCJ 205332, BJS Web, December 2005.

[a] Court of Federal Regulations (CFR) operated by the Bureau of Indian Affairs (BIA).

[b] Tribes that rely on state court for jusidical services (e.g., felony courts, court-ordered treatment, and child support enforcement).

**Table 3.2. State prosecutors' offices with jurisdiction for crimes committed in Indian country, by P.L. 280 status and state, 2007**

| | All prosecutors' offices in P.L. 280 states* | Number of offices— With jurisdiction for felony cases occurring in Indian country under P.L. 280 | Prosecuting at least one felony case |
|---|---|---|---|
| All P.L. 280 states | 672 | 93 | 68 |
| Mandatory states | 294 | 56 | 47 |
| Alaska | 1 | 1 | -- |
| California | 48 | 23 | 21 |
| Minnesota | 76 | 15 | 15 |
| Nebraska | 81 | 3 | 1 |
| Oregon | 31 | 7 | 4 |
| Wisconsin | 57 | 7 | 6 |
| Optional states | 378 | 37 | 21 |
| Arizona | 11 | 1 | 1 |
| Florida | 16 | 1 | 1 |
| Idaho | 34 | 6 | 4 |
| Iowa | 93 | 1 | 1 |
| Montana | 46 | 5 | 1 |
| Nevada | 15 | 2 | 0 |
| North Dakota | 43 | 2 | 1 |
| South Dakota | 58 | 1 | 1 |
| Utah | 26 | 3 | 2 |
| Washington | 36 | 15 | 9 |

Note: The 2007 Census of State Court Prosecutors included 2,330 offices, 66% (1,548) of which were located in states not affected by P.L. 280, and therefore were excluded from all analyses.

-- No information reported.

* Excludes data missing for 110 offices.

In 2007, 19% of all state prosecutors' offices in mandatory P.L. 280 states reported jurisdiction for felony cases occurring in Indian country.

P.L. 280 permitted other states to acquire either complete or partial jurisdiction over crimes committed in Indian country at their option: Arizona, Florida, Idaho, Iowa, Montana, Nevada, North Dakota, South Dakota, Utah, and Washington. Ten percent of all prosecutors' offices in optional P.L. 280 states reported jurisdiction for felony cases in Indian country in 2007.

### *About Three-Quarters of Offices with P.L. 280 Jurisdiction Prosecuted a Felony Case from Indian Country in 2007*

Sixty-eight of the 93 prosecutors' offices with jurisdiction in Indian country reported prosecuting at least one felony case committed in Indian country in 2007. Forty-seven offices in mandatory P.L. 280 states reported prosecuting at least one offense committed in Indian country, and 21 offices in optional P.L. 280 states reported prosecuting at least one offense committed in Indian country in 2007.

Most offices in mandatory P.L. 280 states with jurisdiction for felony offenses in Indian country also reported prosecuting at least one drug-related crime (42 of 56 offices), domestic violence offense (40), aggravated assault (38), parole or probation violation (31), or a crime involving sexual assault or sexual abuse (30) (figure 3.2).

Offices in mandatory P.L. 280 states with jurisdiction for Indian country also reported prosecuting serious felony offenses, including 18 offices that prosecuted at least one rape committed in Indian country and 12 offices that prosecuted a homicide.

### *Prosecutors' Offices with Jurisdiction in Indian Country Had an Average of 16 Assistant Prosecutors on Staff*

The 2007 National Census of State Prosecutors collected operational and administrative information from state prosecutors' offices, including budgets, staffing, and caseload. Offices reporting jurisdiction for crimes committed under P.L. 280 were not asked to disaggregate office resources or operations by whether they were directed toward crimes committed in Indian country or elsewhere in the judicial district.

The census asked respondents to provide or estimate the total number of felony cases closed in 2007. The survey did not ask respondents to provide information on the number of cases that arose from crimes committed in Indian country. This section describes the entire operations of the state prosecutors' offices reporting jurisdiction under P.L. 280, not operations specific to crimes committed in Indian country.

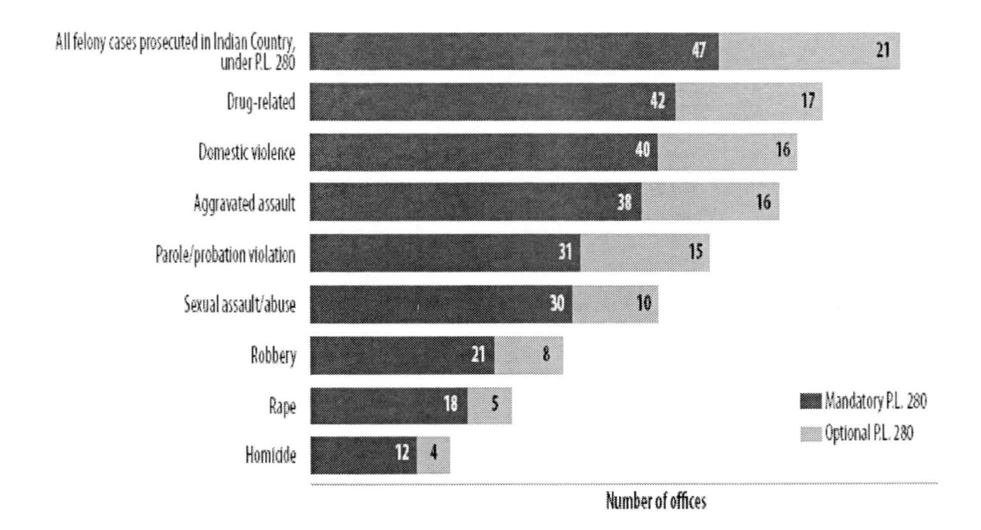


Figure 3.2. State prosecutors' offices reporting prosecution of specific crimes in Indian country, by P.L. 280 status, 2007.

Most (71) state prosecutors' offices that reported jurisdiction for felony cases occurring in Indian country under P.L. 280 served judicial districts with populations of less than 100,000 residents or were part-time offices. In mandatory P.L. 280 states, 7 of the 56 offices with jurisdiction in Indian country served districts with 250,000 or more residents (table 3.3).

Offices with jurisdiction for felony crimes committed in Indian country had an average 2007 budget of $5.2 million, or an expenditure of about $31 per district resident. The median budget was $722,000. The office staff included an average of 16 assistant prosecutors, 3 victim advocates, 4 legal services staff, and 19 support staff (table 3.4).

Offices in mandatory P.L. 280 states reported an average of 61 total staff, including 19 assistant prosecutors, 8 investigators, and 22 support staff. Offices in optional P.L. 280 states reported an average of 38 total staff, 11 assistant prosecutors, 1 investigator, and 14 support staff.

Offices in mandatory P.L. 280 states, reported closing a similar number of felony cases in 2007 compared to optional state offices. State prosecutors' offices in optional P.L. 280 states closed 1,784 felony cases in 2007, while offices in mandatory P.L. 280 states closed 1,699 felony cases.

**Table 3.3. Type of state prosecutors' offices reporting jurisdiction in Indian country, by P.L. 280 status, 2007**

| | | P.L. 280 Status | |
|---|---|---|---|
| Population served | Total | Mandatory | Optional |
| All offices | 93 | 56 | 37 |
| Full-time offices serving a judicial district with— | | | |
| 1 million or more residents | 4 | 2 | 2 |
| 250,000 to 999,999 | 5 | 5 | 0 |
| 100,000 to 249,999 | 13 | 8 | 5 |
| 99,999 or fewer | 65 | 37 | 28 |
| Part-time offices* | 6 | 4 | 2 |

*Part-time offices are defined as those that reported a part-time chief prosecutor in 2007.

## Methodology

The 2007 National Census of State Court Prosecutors (NCSP-07) surveyed 2,330 chief prosecutors in the United States who handled felony cases in state courts of general jurisdiction. The census did not include municipal attorneys or county attorneys who primarily operate in courts of limited jurisdiction. This report describes characteristics of offices that reported jurisdiction for crimes committed in Indian country under P.L. 280 in 2007. Most (66%) state court prosecutors' offices included in the 2007 census were in states not affected by P.L. 280 and are excluded from this report.

The operational and administrative characteristics described in this report represent the functions of the entire office and are not restricted to those functions, staff, budget, or other resources specifically devoted to crimes committed in Indian country, unless otherwise noted.

### *Data Imputations*

BJS relied on previously reported data and valid office characteristics to impute values for critical variables where missing. These critical variables, found in Table 3.4, include the total operating budget, total staff, full- or part-time status of chief prosecutor, number of assistant prosecutors, and number of felony cases closed. Critical variables that were missing in 2007 were imputed from the same office's response to the 2001 Census of State Prosecutors wherever possible.

**Table 3.4. Budget, staffing, and caseload of state prosecutors' offices, by P.L. 280 status, 2007**

| | Total | | P.L. 280 status | | | |
|---|---|---|---|---|---|---|
| | | | Mandatory | | Optional | |
| | Mean | Median | Mean | Median | Mean | Median |
| Total resident population served | 156,495 | 28,893 | 177,407 | 28,965 | 124,846 | 28,606 |
| Total operating budget | $5,173,831 | $722,208 | $6,560,838 | $735,735 | $3,074,577 | $670,000 |
| Budget per resident population served | $31 | $26 | $35 | $27 | $25 | $24 |
| Total staff[a] | 51 | 12 | 61 | 12 | 38 | 12 |
| Chief prosecutor | 1 | 1 | 1 | 1 | 1 | 1 |
| Assistant prosecutors | 16 | 3 | 19 | 4 | 11 | 3 |
| Civil prosecutors | 2 | 0 | 1 | 0 | 4 | 1 |
| Supervisors | 2 | 1 | 2 | 0 | 2 | 1 |
| Managers | 1 | 0 | 1 | 0 | 0 | 0 |
| Victim advocates | 3 | 1 | 3 | 1 | 2 | 1 |
| Legal services | 4 | 0 | 3 | 0 | 4 | 1 |
| Investigators | 5 | 0 | 8 | 0 | 1 | 0 |
| Support staff | 19 | 3 | 22 | 4 | 14 | 3 |
| Felony cases closed[b] | 1,733 | 300 | 1,699 | 300 | 1,784 | 275 |

Note: Statistics include imputed data for some offices. Data were missing for 3 offices that did not provide total operating budget, 1 office that did not provide staffing information, and 6 offices that did not provide the number of felony cases closed. See *Methodology* for more information.

[a] All staff statistics are presented as full-time equivalent staff, calculated as the number of full-time staff plus 50% of the number of half time staff.

[b] Includes all cases charged as a felony that had a judgment of conviction, acquittal, or dismissal, with or without prejudice, entered by the court. Cases closed include all felony cases closed by the prosecutors' offices and include an unknown number of cases committed in Indian country.

For each jurisdiction with valid 2001 and 2007 data, an adjustment ratio was calculated as the ratio of the critical variable's 2001 value to its 2007 value. All ratios greater than the 90th percentile were discarded for imputation purposes. For those offices missing 2007 data, a hot deck imputation procedure was employed to impute the adjustment ratio value from the office's nearest neighbor in terms of state and population size. Where there were no suitable donors in the same state, a donor of similar population size was used. The 2001 data were then adjusted using the imputed adjustment ratio to create the imputed 2007 value for the critical variable where missing. This procedure was followed for 3 offices missing total operating budget, 1 office missing staffing information, and 6 offices missing the number of felony cases closed.

## Reference

Census of Tribal Justice Agencies in Indian Country, 2002, NCJ 205332, BJS Web, `December 2005.

# Selected Findings: Jails in Indian Country, 2009

*Todd D. Minton, BJS Statistician*

At midyear 2009, a total of 2,176 inmates were confined in Indian country jails, a 1.9% increase from the 2,135 inmates confined at midyear 2008 (figure 4.1). This count was based on data from 80 facilities, including jails, confinement facilities, detention centers, and other correctional facilities, that were in operation in Indian country at midyear 2009. For 2008, the number of inmates was based on data for 82 facilities in operation at midyear 2008. The number of inmates held in Indian country jails between 2004 and 2009 increased by 25% from 1,745 inmates to 2,176.

### *The Number of Jails in Indian Country Has Increased between 2004 and 2009*

The Bureau of Justice Statistics (BJS) collected data from 68 correctional facilities in Indian country in 2004, from 79 in 2007, 82 in 2008, and 80 in 2009. The survey was not conducted in 2005 and 2006. Over the 5-year period, a number of facilities closed and new facilities became operational. Eleven facilities permanently closed between 2004 and 2009, and a total of 21 facilities were newly constructed. BJS estimated inmate population counts for

7 facilities in 2004 and 4 facilities in 2007 that did not respond to the surveys. All known operating facilities responded to the 2008 and 2009 surveys. (See *Methodology* for additional details on facility counts and participation in the surveys.) (See *Methodology* in *Jails in Indian Country, 2009*, NCJ 232223, BJS Web, February 2010, for additional details on facility counts and participation in the surveys.)

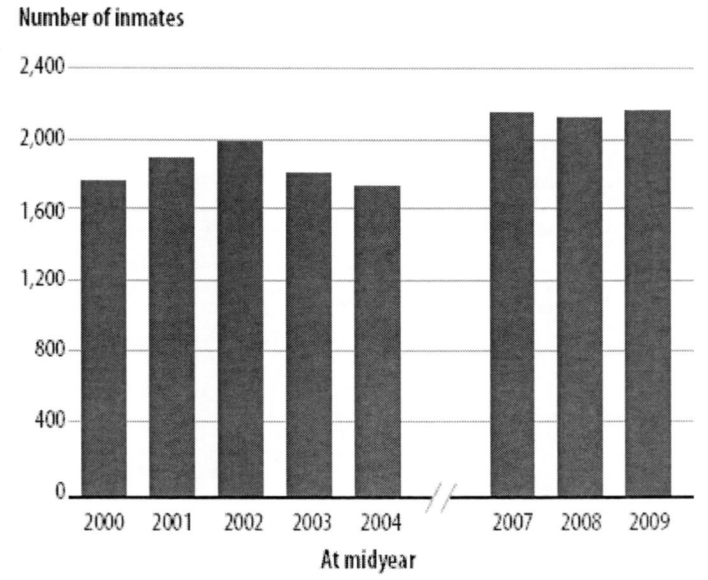


Note: The Survey of Jails in Indian Country was not conducted in 2005 and 2006. Midyear count is the number of inmates held on the last weekday in June.

Figure 4.1. Inmates confined in Indian country jails, midyear 2000-2004 and 2007-2009.

### *On an Average Day in June, the Percentage of Occupied Bed Space Increased from 64.2% to 73.5%*

At midyear 2009, the 80 jail facilities in Indian country were rated to hold 2,891 inmates, down from 2,963 in 82 facilities during the same period in 2008 (table 4.1). The average daily population (ADP) in June—the population measure used to calculate percent of capacity occupied—increased by nearly 12%, from 1,903 inmates (June 2008) to 2,124 (June 2009), while the capacity to hold inmates decreased by 2%. Consequently, the percentage of rated capacity occupied in Indian country jails increased from 64% to 73% during the period.

On June 30, 2009, the 80 facilities held a total of 2,176 inmates and were operating at 75% of rated capacity, remaining relatively stable since 2007. From June 2004 to June 2009, the overall number of beds (or rated capacity) grew at a faster rate (34%) than the the inmate population (25%).

***Small Number of Jails Held More than Half of the Inmate Population***

Eleven jails held more than half (51%) of the total inmate population at midyear 2009 (table 4.2). Between midyear 2008 and midyear 2009, the population in these jails increased by 247 inmates (29%). In 2008, 9 of the 11 facilities held the majority of jail inmates in Indian country.

**Table 4.1. Inmates, rated capacity, and percent of capacity occupied in Indian country jails, 2004 and 2007–2009**

| | 2004 | 2007 | 2008 | 2009 |
|---|---|---|---|---|
| Number of inmates | | | | |
| Midyear[a] | 1,745 | 2,163 | 2,135 | 2,176 |
| ADP[b] | 1,622 | 2,046 | 1,903 | 2,124 |
| Rated capacity | 2,162 | 2,900 | 2,963 | 2,891 |
| Percent of capacity occupied[c] | | | | |
| Midyear | 80.7% | 74.6% | 72.1% | 75.3% |
| ADP | 75.0 | 70.6 | 64.2 | 73.5 |
| Number of operating facilities | 68 | 79 | 82 | 80 |

[a] Midyear count is the number of inmates held on the last weekday in June.

[b] Average daily population (ADP) is the sum of the number of inmates held on each day in June, divided by 30.

[c] Population as a percent of capacity occupied is calculated by dividing the population count of a facility by its rated capacity and multiplying by 100.

Over the 365-day period, 6 jails that held the majority of inmates in Indian country in 2008 experienced large declines in their jail populations. The combined decrease in the size of the jail population in these facilities was 33% (90 inmates) from midyear 2008 to midyear 2009.

Among the 11 facilities holding the majority of inmates in 2009, the Gila River Department of Rehabilitation and Supervision - Adult facility reported the largest decline (30 inmates or 17%) in the number of jail inmates. The jail population in this facility has decreased by 92 inmates (38%) from its peak of 241 inmates reported at midyear 2007.

**Table 4.2. Jails in Indian country that held the majority of inmates in 2009 compared to 2008, by facility**

| | Custody population at midyear* | | Change in population | |
|---|---|---|---|---|
| Facility | 2008 | 2009 | Number | Percent |
| Total, 11 facilities | 859 | 1,106 | 247 | 29% |
| Tohono O'odham Adult Detention Center (AZ) | 137 | 192 | 55 | 40% |
| Gila River Department of Rehabilitation and Supervision - Adult (AZ) | 179 | 149 | -30 | -17 |
| San Carlos Department of Corrections and Rehabilitation - Adult and Juvenile Detention (AZ) | 88 | 147 | 59 | 67 |
| Truxton Canyon Adult Detention Center (AZ) | 39 | 105 | 66 | 169 |
| White Mountain Apache Detention Center (AZ) | 101 | 95 | -6 | -6 |
| Oglala Sioux Tribal Offenders Facility (SD) | 52 | 95 | 43 | 83 |
| Standing Rock Law Enforcement and Adult Detention Center (ND) | 71 | 93 | 22 | 31 |
| Nisqually Adult Corrections (WA) | 59 | 73 | 14 | 24 |
| Menominee Tribal Detention Facility (WI) | 54 | 53 | -1 | -2 |
| Navajo Department of Corrections - Shiprock Police Department and Adult Detention (NM) | 46 | 52 | 6 | 13 |
| Laguna Tribal Police and Detention Center (NM) | 33 | 52 | 19 | 58 |

Note: Based on facilities that held the most inmates on June 30, 2009.
*Midyear count is the number of inmates held on the last weekday in June.

Two facilities, the Truxton Canyon Adult Detention Center and the Laguna Tribal Police and Detention Center, were among the 11 facilities holding the majority of jail inmates in 2009. These 2 facilities were not among the 11 facilities holding the majority of inmates in 2008. (See *Jails in Indian Country, 2008*, BJS Web, December 2008.)

The Truxton Canyon Adult Detention Center reported the largest increase in the inmate population (66 inmates or 169%) between midyear 2008 and midyear 2009. The Laguna Tribal Police and Detention Center increased by 58% (19 inmates) between 2008 and 2009.

Based on the 80 facilities responding to the survey in both 2008 and 2009, the overall change in the inmate population (up 45 inmates) was relatively small. Thirty-three facilities, which were mostly the larger facilities, accounted for this increase (not shown in table).

Change in the size of the jail population in Indian country was varied. More than half of the 80 jails experienced either a decline (40 jails) or no change (7 jails) in the size of their inmate population over the 12-month period ending midyear 2009. Overall, the 50% increase (415 inmates) in the jail population in 33 jails was offset by a 30% decline (370 inmates) in 40 jails.

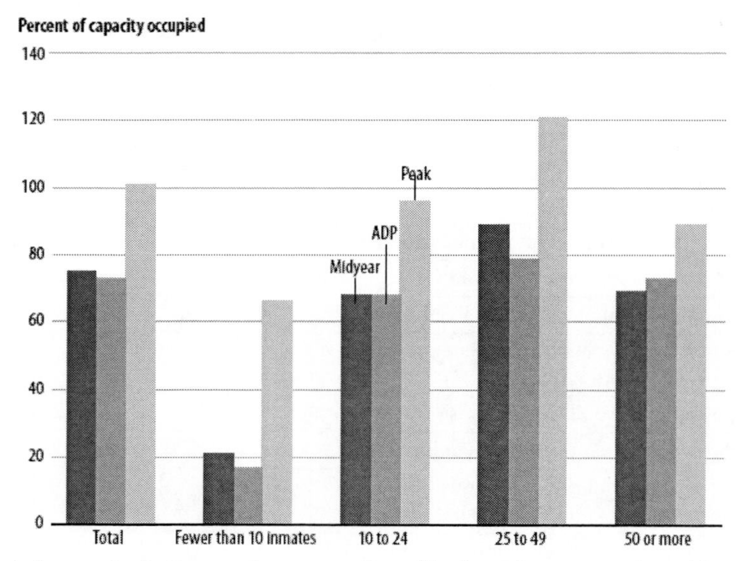


Note: Rated capacity is the maximum number of beds or inmates assigned by a rating official. Midyear count is the number of inmates held on the last weekday in June. Average daily population (ADP) is the sum of the number of inmates held on each day in June divided by 30. Peak population is the population held on the day in June in which the custody population of a facility was the largest.

Figure 4.2. Rated capacity occupied, by type of inmate count, June 2009.

### *The Use of Jail Space Varied by Facility Size*

Indian country jails rated to hold 25 to 49 inmates were operating at 89% of their rated capacity on June 30, 2009, and at 79% on an average day in June. An average day in June was based on the ADP, or the sum of the numbers held on each day in June divided by 30. In contrast, the lowest percentage of capacity occupied during June 2009 was among the 11 small jails rated to hold fewer than 10 inmates. These facilities were operating at

21% of rated capacity at midyear and at 17% of capacity on an average day in June 2009 (figure 4.2).

**Table 4.3. Number of Indian country jails, by percent of rated capacity occupied, June 2009**

| | Number of jails | | |
|---|---|---|---|
| Percent of capacity occupied[a] | Midyear[b] | ADP[c] | Peak[d] |
| Less than 25% | 17 | 20 | 7 |
| 25-49% | 15 | 11 | 8 |
| 50-74% | 19 | 21 | 15 |
| 75-100% | 11 | 15 | 12 |
| More than 100% | 18 | 13 | 38 |

[a] Population as a percent of capacity occupied is calculated by dividing the population count of a facility by its rated capacity and multiplying by 100.
[b] Midyear count is the number of inmates held on the last weekday in June.
[c] Average daily population (ADP) is the sum of the number of inmates held on each day in June, divided by 30.
[d] Peak population is the population held on the day in June in which the custody population of a facility was the largest.

Compared to facilities in all other size categories, the large jails with a rated capacity of 50 or more inmates reported the only increase in occupied bed space between 2008 and 2009. The percentage of capacity occupied in these jails increased from 51% to 69% during the 12 months ending at midyear 2009, and from 49% to 73% on an average day in June 2008 and 2009.

The amount of bed space occupied was also measured based on a facility's most crowded day in June. Nearly half (38 facilities) of the 80 facilities in Indian country were operating above rated capacity on the most crowded day in June (table 4.3). Of those facilities, 18 were operating above rated capacity on June 30, and 13 were operating above rated capacity on an average day during June 2009.

### *High Volumes of Admissions of Inmates Were Processed through Indian Country Jails*

Eighty Indian country jails admitted 11,357 persons during June 2009, up slightly from 11,149 admissions in 81 facilities during June 2008 (table 4.4). The number of admissions grew by 1.6% in the 79 facilities that reported data on admissions in both June 2009 (11,323) and June 2008 (11,147) (not shown in table).

Admissions to facilities rated to hold between 25 to 49 inmates accounted for about 48% (5,503) of all admissions in June 2009, down from 59% of all admissions in June 2008. The largest Indian country jails accounted for less than 20% of all facilities and reported a total increase of nearly 75% in the number of jail admissions during the 12-month period. Admissions to the largest Indian country jails increased from 1,915 inmates to 3,342 from June 2008 to June 2009. The 15 jails rated to hold 50 or more inmates had the highest average number of admissions per month (233), compared to jails in all other size categories (not shown in table).

### *Inmate Deaths and Attempted Suicides in Indian Country Jails Declined*

Indian country jail authorities reported no deaths in custody between July 1, 2008, and June 30, 2009, down from 4 reported deaths during the 12-month period ending June 30, 2008. Attempted suicides by inmates declined from 78 in 2008 to 56 in 2009.

### *Expected Length of Stay Was 5.6 Days for Indian Country Jail Inmates in June 2009*

During June 2009, the expected average length of stay for inmates confined in Indian country jails was 5.6 days, up from 5.1 days during June 2008. Length of stay is the time held in custody from admission to release. The expected length of stay for inmates was the highest (9.1 days) in facilities that were rated to hold 50 or more inmates, down from 10.3 days in June 2008. Inmates held in jails rated to hold less than 10 inmates experienced the shortest expected length of stay (2.1 days).

### *Inmate Characteristics Remain Relatively Unchanged; The Number Held for Domestic Violence Declined*

Inmate characteristics by sex, age, and offense have changed in absolute numbers since 2000 (table 4.5). However, the distribution within most categories remained stable between 2000 and 2008, with a change in the distribution of inmates by sex, conviction status, and offense type at midyear 2009.

Adult males accounted for the largest portion of the inmate population in Indian country jails during the decade. The female jail population had small but steady increases from midyear 2000 to 2008, with a nearly 8% decrease in the size of this population between midyear 2008 and midyear 2009. Except for one juvenile female inmate, the decline was entirely among the adult female jail population.

The percentage of convicted inmates increased from 57% in 2002 to 69% in 2009. Inmates confined for a violent offense made up about 37% of the jail population at midyear 2009, down from 41% at midyear 2008. Most (75%) of this decline was among the population held for domestic violence. Domestic violence (12%) and simple or aggravated assault (15%) accounted for the largest percentage of violent offenders held in 2009, followed by unspecified violent offenses (8%) and rape or sexual assault (2%).

Since peaking at midyear 2007, the percentage of inmates held for domestic violence has steadily declined, from 20% in 2007 to 12% in 2009. The Gila River Department of Rehabilitation and Supervision - Adult accounted for a large portion of the decline in domestic violence offenders between 2007 and 2009.

**Table 4.4. Admissions and expected length of stay in Indian country jails during June, by facility size, June 2009**

| Facility size[a] | Number of facilities | ADP[b] | Estimated June admissions | Expected average length of stay[c] |
|---|---|---|---|---|
| Total | 80 | 2,124 | 11,357 | 5.6 days |
| Fewer than 10 inmates | 11 | 9 | 133 | 2.1 |
| 10 to 24 | 24 | 276 | 2,379 | 3.5 |
| 25 to 49 | 30 | 820 | 5,503 | 4.5 |
| 50 or more | 15 | 1,018 | 3,342 | 9.1 |

Note: Detail may not sum to total due to rounding.

[a] Based on the rated capacity, the maximum number of beds or inmates assigned by a rating official.

[b] Average daily population (ADP) is the sum of the number of inmates held on each day in June, divided by 30.

[c] Expected length of stay was calculated by dividing the average daily population (ADP) by the number of June admissions, and multiplying by 30. See *Methodology* in *Jails in Indian Country, 2009* for details on estimating expected length of stay.

**Table 4.5. Number of inmates confined in Indian country jails, by demographic characteristic, conviction status, and offense, midyear 2002, 2004, and 2007–2009**

| | Number of inmates held at midyear[a] | | | | | | Percent of inmates held at midyear | | | | | |
|---|---|---|---|---|---|---|---|---|---|---|---|---|
| Characteristic | 2000 | 2002 | 2004 | 2007 | 2008 | 2009 | 2000 | 2002 | 2004 | 2007 | 2008 | 2009 |
| Total | 1,775 | 2,006 | 1,745 | 1,996 | 2,135 | 2,176 | 100% | 100% | 100% | 100% | 100% | 100% |
| Sex | | | | | | | | | | | | |
| Male | 1,421 | 1,618 | 1,346 | 1,582 | 1,678 | 1,754 | 80% | 81% | 77% | 79% | 79% | 81% |
| Female | 354 | 388 | 398 | 414 | 457 | 422 | 20 | 19 | 23 | 21 | 21 | 19 |
| Age group/sex Adults | 1,498 | 1,699 | 1,546 | 1,743 | 1,882 | 1,919 | 84% | 85% | 89% | 87% | 88% | 88% |
| Male | 1,214 | 1,399 | 1,222 | 1,415 | 1,498 | 1,571 | 68 | 70 | 70 | 71 | 70 | 72 |
| Female | 284 | 300 | 324 | 328 | 384 | 348 | 16 | 15 | 19 | 16 | 18 | 16 |
| Juveniles | 277 | 307 | 198 | 253 | 253 | 257 | 16 | 15 | 11 | 13 | 12 | 12 |
| Male | 207 | 219 | 124 | 167 | 180 | 183 | 12 | 11 | 7 | 8 | 8 | 8 |
| Female | 70 | 88 | 74 | 86 | 73 | 74 | 4 | 4 | 4 | 4 | 3 | 3 |
| Conviction status | | | | | | | | | | | | |
| Convicted | 1,072 | 1,120 | 966 | 1,116 | 1,340 | 1,496 | 61% | 57% | 58% | 59% | 63% | 69% |
| Unconvicted | 689 | 857 | 697 | 763 | 776 | 680 | 39 | 43 | 42 | 41 | 37 | 31 |

| Type of offense | | | | | | | | | | | | |
|---|---|---|---|---|---|---|---|---|---|---|---|---|
| | Number of inmates held at midyear[a] | | | | | | Percent of inmates held at midyear | | | | | |
| Characteristic | 2000 | 2002 | 2004 | 2007 | 2008 | 2009 | 2000 | 2002 | 2004 | 2007 | 2008 | 2009 |
| Domestic violence | ... | 291 | 257 | 362 | 307 | 252 | ...% | 15% | 18% | 20% | 15% | 12% |
| Assault | ... | ... | 190 | 233 | 308 | 299 | ... | ... | 13 | 13 | 15 | 15 |
| Rape or sexual assault | ... | ... | 34 | 45 | 42 | 42 | ... | ... | 2 | 2 | 2 | 2 |
| Other violence | ... | ... | 79 | 108 | 177 | 168 | ... | ... | 6 | 6 | 9 | 8 |
| DWI/DUI[b] | 274 | 226 | 195 | 137 | 184 | 229 | 17 | 11 | 14 | 8 | 9 | 11 |
| Drug law violation | 133 | 126 | 104 | 132 | 104 | 107 | 8 | 6 | 7 | 7 | 5 | 5 |
| Other | ... | ... | 569 | 804 | 954 | 955 | ... | ... | 40 | 44 | 46 | 47 |
| Offense not reported | ... | ... | 317 | 175 | 59 | 124 | / | / | / | / | / | / |

Note: Detailed characteristics may not be equal to the total number of confined inmates because of incomplete data. See appendix tables 1-3 in *Jails in Indian Country, 2009,* NCJ 232223, BJS Web, February 2011, for a list of all facilities and inmate characteristics.

[a] Midyear count is the number of inmates held on the last weekday in June.

[b] Includes driving while intoxicated and driving while under the influence of drugs or alcohol.

... Not collected.

/ Not reported.

## SUMMARY: TRIBAL YOUTH IN THE FEDERAL JUSTICE SYSTEM

*Mark Motivans, Ph.D., and Howard Snyder, Ph.D., BJS Statisticians*

The federal criminal justice response to tribal youth varies by the state in which the offense occurred, the nature of the offense, the availability of community-and confinement-based services, and discretionary decisions made by tribal, state, and federal justice agencies. Cases involving tribal youth in the federal system may result in 1) a delinquency adjudication and court-ordered supervision and out-of-home placement, or 2) the youth being transferred to adult status and prosecuted and sentenced as an adult.

This summary describes the federal response to tribal youth during the case-processing stages from investigation to corrections. In this report, a federal juvenile delinquent is a person who has committed an offense while under age 18, and the federal prosecutor has certified a federal basis for jurisdiction. Juvenile and youth are used interchangeably in this report.

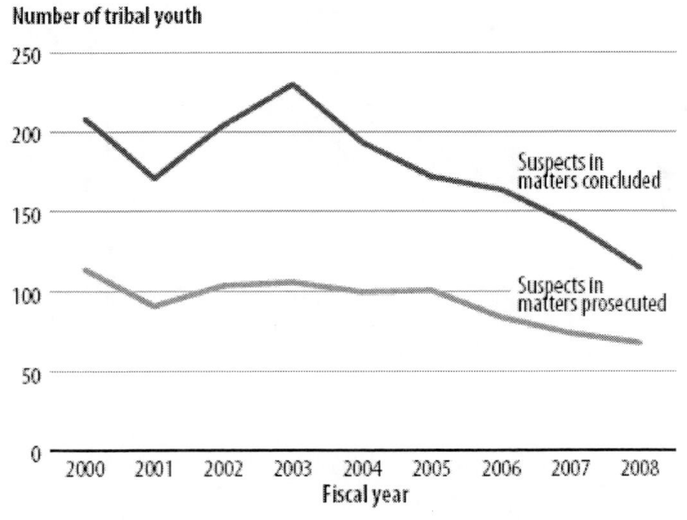


Source: Urban Institute analysis. See *Methodology* for more information.

Figure 5.1. Tribal youth in matters concluded and in matters prosecuted by U.S. attorneys, 2000–2008.

The number of tribal youth in matters concluded by federal prosecutors and the total number of tribal youth prosecuted decreased from 2003 to 2008 (figure 5.1). Tribal youth in matters concluded by federal prosecutors dropped to 115 in 2008, down from 230 in 2003.

Findings presented in this report are mostly from a recent study conducted by The Urban Institute under a cooperative agreement with the Bureau of Justice Statistics (BJS). The study was also sponsored by the Office of Juvenile Justice and Delinquency Prevention (OJJDP).

## HIGHLIGHTS

- In 2008, relatively few juveniles were referred to federal prosecutors (315 out of 178,570 suspects) or admitted to federal prison jurisdiction (156 out 71,663 offenders).
- Tribal youth (70) comprised nearly half of juveniles (152) handled by the federal courts in 2008.
- Federal judicial districts of Arizona, Montana, South Dakota, New Mexico, and North Dakota accounted for 94% of tribal youth investigated, 92% of those prosecuted, and 88% of those admitted to federal prison jurisdiction in 2008.
- In 2008, about 72% of tribal youth were investigated for violent offenses, including sexual abuse (35%), assault (20%), and murder (17%).
- About 40% of matters involving tribal youth were declined by federal prosecutors in 2008.
- A greater share of cases involving tribal youth in U.S. district courts were terminated by conviction (91%) than by dismissal (9%).
- From 1994 to 2008, the lowest number of tribal (72) and non-tribal youth (84) admitted to the jurisdiction of federal prison authorities occurred in 2008.
- Admissions to federal prison jurisdiction among tribal youth declined 10% per year from 1999 to 2008, while non-tribal youth admissions declined 12% per year.
- In 2008, tribal youth served an average of 26 months under federal jurisdiction, which was more than double the tribal justice system maximum sentence of 12 months.

## Tracking tribal youth through the stage of the federal criminal case process

The federal criminal justice system is not currently well-equipped to monitor how tribal juvenile offenders are processed across stages. There is a lack of unified, system-wide data standards in reporting how youth—especially tribal youth—are handled in the federal system. Juveniles or offenses committed in Indian country are not systematically tracked across the federal justice agencies. Researchers have to devise analytic methods to identify tribal youth using administrative data from each criminal justice stage (arrest, sentencing, and corrections).

## How is federal jurisdiction over tribal juvenile delinquents determined?

The determination of jurisdiction over offenses occurring in Indian country is first subject to whether state courts have jurisdiction based on Public Law 280 (P.L. 280).[1] If a state has P. L. 280 status, jurisdiction over offenses occurring in Indian country lies with the state or tribal courts, not the federal courts. The determination of whether federal jurisdiction applies next depends on the offender and victim in the crime:

- If the offender is a juvenile tribal member and the victim is also a tribal member, and the offense is 1 of 15 crimes covered by the Major Crimes Act then jurisdiction is with both the tribal and federal courts.[2]
- If the offender is a juvenile tribal member and the victim is a non-tribal member, and the crime is covered by the Major Crimes Act or federal enclave status, then federal and tribal courts have shared jurisdiction. The Assimilative Crimes Act permits state law to be applied in federal court where the Major Crimes Act does not apply but federal interest exists.
- If the crime involves a non-tribal offender and a tribal member victim, then federal courts have exclusive jurisdiction.

[1] Congress passed Public Law 280 in 1953, which relinquishes the federal government of criminal and civil jurisdiction in certain states and places jurisdiction with those states.

[2] The Major Crimes Act provides federal jurisdiction over certain offenses committed by tribal members. (See Title 18 U.S.C. §§ 1152, 1153.)

Once federal jurisdiction has been established, the Federal Juvenile Delinquency Act (FJDA) provides the procedures to bring the tribal youth to federal court.

A federal juvenile delinquent is defined as a person who has committed an offense while less than 18 years old, but has not reached age 21 at sentencing. Juvenile and youth are used interchangeably in this report.

**How are juveniles handled in the federal justice system?**

Most juveniles, or persons under age 18, in the United States are handled in state or local courts, which have a separate juvenile justice system, rather than in the federal courts. Federal law permits handling of juveniles in the federal system only in limited circumstances. Apart from those committing crimes in Indian country or on military bases, juveniles that commit offenses as members of drug trafficking gangs, violent criminal gangs, or other federal offenses may be subject to federal jurisdiction. In these cases, the U.S. attorney for each district must certify to the district court that (1) the juvenile court or court of a state does not have jurisdiction or refuses to assume jurisdiction; 2) the state does not have available programs or services adequate for the needs of juveniles; or 3) the offense charged is a felony crime of violence or specified drug offenses, and there is substantial federal interest in the case.

**In what circumstances are tribal and non-tribal juveniles transferred to adult status (for prosecution and sentencing as an adult rather than a juvenile delinquent)?**

Once federal jurisdiction has been determined and certification of delinquency established, a transfer hearing establishes the status of juveniles as to whether they will be transferred for prosecution as an adult. Felony crimes of violence or drug or firearm offenses trigger eligibility for adult transfer with certain age restrictions. Age thirteen is the minimum age for transfer to adult status for murder and assault, and for robbery, bank robbery, or aggravated sexual abuse with a firearm. An exception is crimes committed in Indian country where the tribe has opted not to permit prosecution of juveniles age 13 as adults.

Age fifteen is the minimum age for transfer to adult status for committing any crime of violence (including physical force against a person or property).

A juvenile can be housed in a Federal Bureau of Prisons (BOP) institution at age 18 if sentenced as an adult. BOP does not operate its own facilities for juveniles; rather, they contract with private entities and state and local governments for both secure and non-secure (community-based) juvenile facilities to house tribal and non-tribal youth under their jurisdiction.

## INVESTIGATION AND PROSECUTION

Tribal police are often the first to respond to a crime in Indian country. Offenses committed by tribal youth may be investigated by a combination of tribal police and federal law enforcement agencies. The federal Bureau of Investigation (FBI) and the Bureau of Indian Affairs (BIA) are the primary federal law enforcement agencies investigating tribal youth matters.

Tribal youth commonly enter the federal justice system with an arrest for a warrant issued on either a complaint or juvenile information (written accusation made by the prosecutor). For serious offenses that may indicate a federal crime, the U.S. attorney's office in the district is notified as is the juvenile's parent/guardian. The juvenile must be taken before a U.S. magistrate as soon as possible, where charges are read and the juvenile is informed of rights. Federal prosecutors next determine if the matter should be adjudicated in federal courts, disposed by U.S. magistrate, or declined for prosecution.

### *In 2008, 4 in 10 Matters Involving a Tribal Youth Were Declined by Federal Prosecutors*

During 2008, 40% of tribal youth in matters concluded were declined for further prosecution, which was lower than the 46% declination rate for non-tribal youth in 2008. However, the average declination rate for tribal youth (45%) was higher than for non-tribal youth (37%) from 2004 to 2008.

The most common reason for declination of tribal youth matters in 2008 was case related (50%) (table 5.1). Case-related reasons included weak evidence, stale case, witness problems, and jurisdiction or venue problems (figure 5.2). Some declined matters involved tribal youth that were subsequently referred to other authorities for prosecution, such as to the tribe or the state where the tribe is located.

The share of declinations for tribal youth that were referred to other authorities or received an alternative resolution increased from 13% of all declinations in 2005 to 20% in 2008. Among non-tribal youth, the most common reason for declination (71%) was that the suspect was a juvenile (not shown in table).

### *Most Tribal Youth in Matters Referred to U.S. Attorneys Were Prosecuted by Federal Prosecutors*

In 2008, 59% of tribal youth who were referred to federal prosecutors were prosecuted, which was higher than the 54% prosecution rate for non-tribal youth in 2008 (including matters disposed by U.S. magistrates). From 2004 to 2008, the averageprosecution rate for tribal youth (55%) was comparable to that of non-tribal youth (53%).

Various factors go into the decision to prosecute a matter, including seriousness of the crime, strength of the evidence, youth's criminal history and drug/alcohol use, tribal capacity to prosecute, and tribal preference. Tribes having concurrent jurisdiction with federal jurisdiction may have limitations on available secure placement options and treatment resources. The potential penalty that could be received if a matter was handled in tribal or state venues may also be considered.[5]

**Table 5.1. Reason for matters declined for prosecution with tribal youth suspects, 2005–2008**

| | | | Reasons for declinations | | | | | |
|---|---|---|---|---|---|---|---|---|
| Fiscal year | Matters concluded | Number of declina-tions | Total | Case-related[a] | Suspect-related[b] | No crime | Referred to other authorities[c] | Other |
| 2005 | 172 | 69 | 100% | 58% | 10% | 9% | 13% | 10% |
| 2006 | 164 | 80 | 100% | 61 | 10 | 10 | 13 | 6 |
| 2007 | 143 | 68 | 100% | 47 | 15 | 10 | 18 | 10 |
| 2008 | 115 | 46 | 100% | 50 | 7 | 15 | 20 | 8 |

[a] Includes weak evidence, stale case, witness problems, or jurisdiction or venue problems.

[b] Includes age of offender and offender 's criminal history and drug/alcohol use.

[c] Includes pretrial alternative resolutions, such as pretrial diversion.

Source: Urban Institute analysis of Executive Office for U.S. Attorneys, National LIONS data base, fiscal years 2005–2008.

---

[5] The Indian Civil Rights Act (Title 25 U.S.C. § 1302(7)), for example, limited tribes in sentencing persons convicted of serious crimes to a maximum of 1 year in jail and a $5,000 fine. Recently, the Tribal Law and Order Act extended the maximum sentence that a tribe can impose to three years.

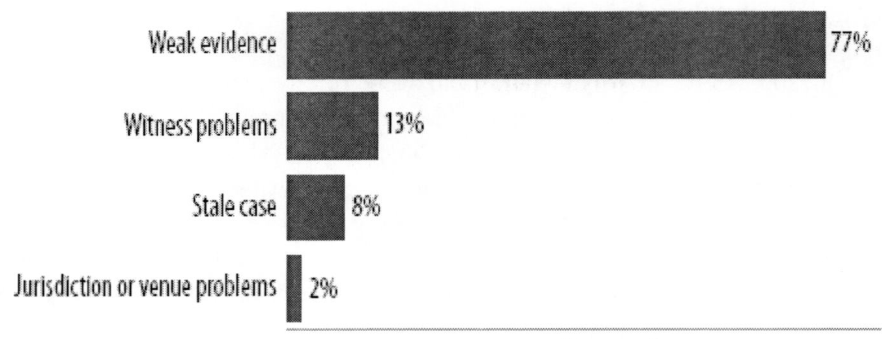


Source: Urban Institute analysis of Executive Office for U.S. Attorneys, National LIONS data base, fiscal years 2005–2008.

Figure 5.2. Case-related reasons for matters declined for prosecution with tribal youth suspects, 2005–2008.

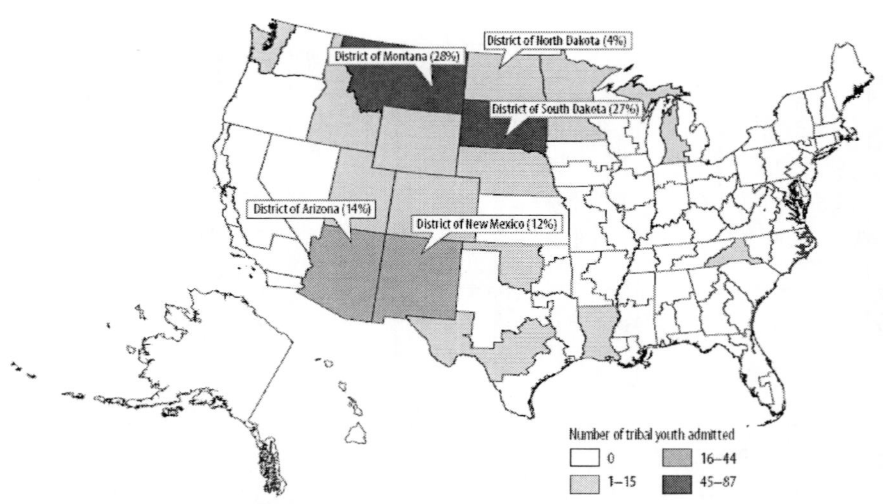


Source: Bureau of Justice Statistics analysis of data from the Federal Bureau of Prisons, SENTRY database, fiscal years 2006–2008.

Figure 5.3. Tribal youth admitted to the jurisdiction of the Federal Bureau of Prisons, and five federal judicial districts that committed the majority of tribal youth, 2006–2008.

**Table 5.2. Federally recognized tribes and enrolled members, 2005**

| Federal judicial district | Tribal entities | | Tribal enrollment | | | Tribal population under age 16 | | |
|---|---|---|---|---|---|---|---|---|
| | Number | Percent | Number | Percent | District rank | Number | Percent of total enrollment | District ranl |
| Total | 590 | 100% | 1,978,099 | 100% | ~ | 503,958 | 100% | ~ |
| Arizona | 22 | 3.7% | 269,778 | 13.6% | 2 | 70,854 | 14.1% | 2 |
| New Mexico | 25 | 4.2 | 174,199 | 8.8 | 3 | 43,234 | 8.6 | 4 |
| South Dakota | 8 | 1.4 | 115,513 | 5.8 | 5 | 27,534 | 5.5 | 6 |
| Montana | 8 | 1.4 | 66,962 | 3.4 | 6 | 14,957 | 3 | 9 |
| North Dakota | 6 | 1 | 58,220 | 2.9 | 8 | 13,851 | 2.7 | 10 |
| All other districts | 521 | 88.3 | 1,293,427 | 65.4 | ~ | 333,528 | 66.2 | ~ |

~Not available.

Source: U.S. Department of the Interior, Bureau of Indian Affairs. *American Indian Population and Labor Force Report, 2005,* available at: http://www.bia.gov/WhatWeDo/Knowledge/Reports/index.htm, calendar year 2005.

**Nearly 9 of 10 tribal youth admitted to Federal Bureau of Prisons jurisdiction from 2006 to 2008 came from five federal judicial districts**

From 2006 to 2008, 85% of tribal youth admitted to the jurisdiction of the Federal Bureau of Prisons (BOP) were from these five federal judicial districts: Arizona, Montana, New Mexico, North Dakota, and South Dakota (figure 5.3).

The most recent tribal population data from the Bureau of Indian Affairs (2005) showed that these five districts contained 12% of the 590 federally recognized tribal entities and 35% of the more than 1.9 million total tribal enrollment population (table 5.2). Thirty-four percent of the enrolled tribal population under age 16 resided on or near reservations in these five federal judicial districts.

## Adjudication and Sentencing

Federal statutes provide for a youth's release pending trial to a parent/ guardian, unless it is determined that detention is necessary to ensure a timely appearance or to ensure safety of juveniles or others (Title 18 U.S.C. § 5034). The federal pretrial services agency oversees supervision of the youth on pretrial release. For juveniles detained, a foster home or community-based facility near the youth's home community is sought. Pretrial juveniles are not to be detained in facilities permitting regular contact with adult offenders nor with other juveniles who have been adjudicated.

## In 2008, 91% of Cases Terminated in U.S. District Court Involving Tribal Youth Resulted in Conviction

Most (91%) tribal youth cases terminated ended in conviction in 2008. Most of the convictions were the result of a guilty plea (88%) than a determination of guilt at trial (3%). In comparison, 95% of non-tribal youth were convicted in 2008, with 91% resulting from guilty pleas and 5% following trial. From 2004 to 2008, the average conviction rate for tribal youth (92%) was higher than for non-tribal youth (87%).

In juvenile adjudication proceedings, the judge has the discretion to impose an out-of-home placement, probation and conditions of probation, or restitution. The youth may also be transferred to adult status and prosecuted and sentenced as an adult.

An adjudicated juvenile can receive up to 3 years of probation. The duration of a sentence for youth adjudicated delinquent to the jurisdiction of federal prison authorities depends on the age of the juvenile at disposition (see text box below). Juveniles under the age of 18 are not allowed to be placed in an institution in which the youth has regular contact with incarcerated adults. A juvenile can be housed in a Federal Bureau of Prisons (BOP) institution at the age of 21 if sentenced as a juvenile.

**The maximum time under federal jurisdiction of juveniles adjudicated delinquent depends on the age at disposition**

- If a juvenile was under 18 years of age at time of disposition, detention may not extend beyond the juvenile reaching age 21 (figure 5.4).
- If a juvenile was between the ages of 18 and 21 at time of disposition, the maximum federal jurisdiction is 5 years.
- Juveniles adjudicated delinquent and under the age of 21 are not to be detained in facilities permitting regular contact with adult convicts. At age 21, however, an adjudicated delinquent can be placed in an adult facility.
- The term that an adjudicated delinquent receives may not exceed the maximum period of imprisonment authorized had the juvenile been an adult. Federal sentencing guidelines do not apply to adjudications of delinquency.

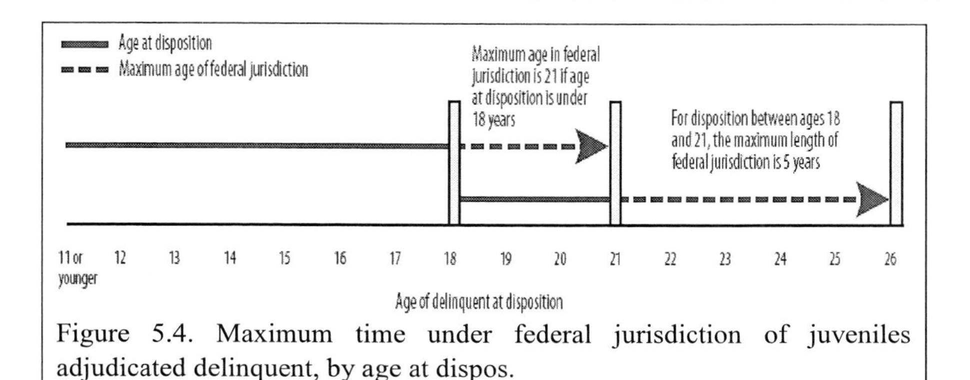


Figure 5.4. Maximum time under federal jurisdiction of juveniles adjudicated delinquent, by age at dispos.

## Corrections

The number of tribal youth admitted to BOP jurisdiction increased from 107 in 1994 to a peak of 252 in 2000— a 136% increase due exclusively to the growth in tribal youth handled as adjudicated delinquents (figure 5.5). The number of tribal youth admitted to the BOP subsequently decreased from 252 in 2000 to 72 in 2008.

In 2008, the number of tribal (72) and non-tribal youth (84) admitted to the jurisdiction of federal prison authorities was the lowest in the period from 1994 to 2008. From 1999 to 2008, the number of tribal youth admissions declined an annual average of 10%, and non-tribal admissions declined at an annual average of 12%. Tribal youth peaked at 252 admissions in 2000, and nontribal youth peaked at 272 admissions in 1999 (figure 5.6).

Most (88%) of the decline in tribal youth from 1999 to 2008 was due to a decrease in youth who had been adjudicated delinquent. Twelve percent of the decline was due to a decrease in tribal youth who had been transferred to adult status. In comparison, most of the decline for non-tribal youth admitted to the BOP over this period was comprised of juveniles who had been transferred to adult status.

In 2008, 72% of tribal youth were admitted to BOP jurisdiction for a violent offense, including sexual abuse (29%), assault (25%), and murder (15%) (table 5.3). Tribal youth admitted for property offenses (mostly burglary) peaked in 2000 (66) and began to decline in 2001, dropping to 14 admissions in 2008. By 2008, tribal youth admitted to BOP jurisdiction for both property and violent offenses had declined to the lowest levels since 1999.

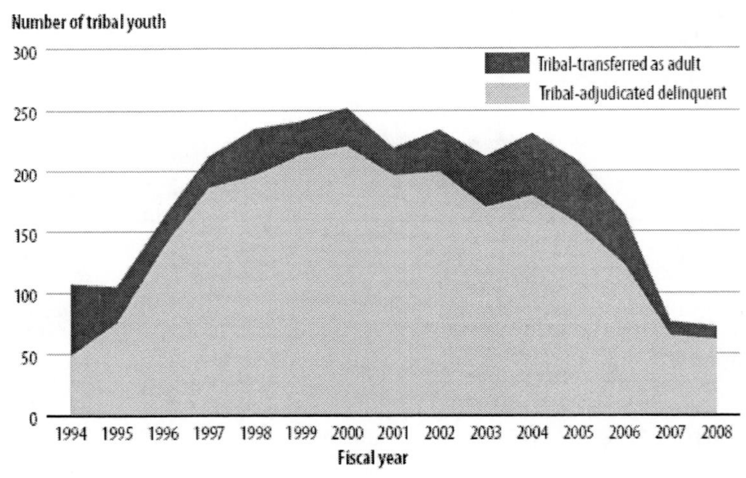


Note: Data for fiscal years 1999–2008 based on Urban Institute analysis of Federal Bureau of Prisons, SENTRY database. Data for fiscal years 1994–1998 based on BJS analysis of SENTRY data.

Figure 5.5. Tribal youth admitted to the jurisdiction of the Federal Bureau of Prisons, by status at admission, 1994–2008.

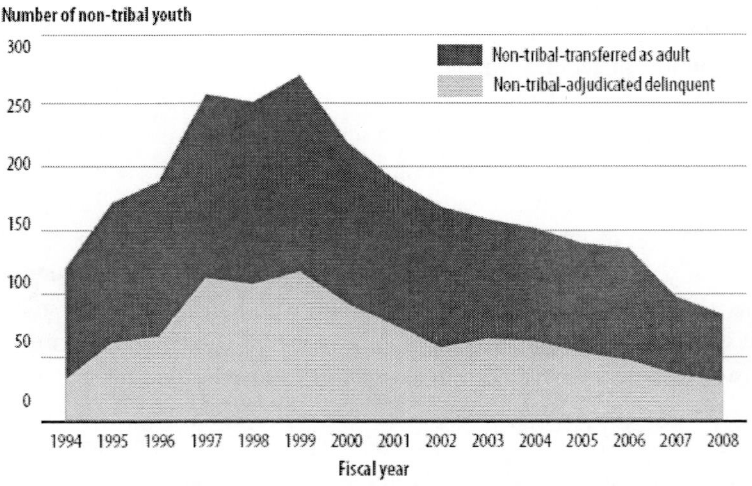


Note: Data for fiscal years 1999–2008 based on Urban Institute analysis of Federal Bureau of Prisons, SENTRY database. Data for fiscal years 1994–1998 based on BJS analysis of SENTRY data.

Figure 5.6. Non-tribal youth admitted to the jurisdiction of the Federal Bureau of Prisons, by status at admission, 1994–2008.

Among non-tribal youth admitted to BOP jurisdiction, violent and drug offenses comprised the majority of offense types (not shown in table). Most tribal youth admitted to BOP jurisdiction from 1999 to 2008 had been adjudicated delinquent (83%), while most non-tribal youth had been prosecuted as adults (65%).

### *At Yearend 2003, 298 Tribal Youth Were in BOP Facilities, Including Both Juvenile Contract and Adult Facilities*

In 2003, 74% of tribal youth were housed under BOP jurisdiction in Minnesota, Arizona, Utah, the Western District of Texas, and Colorado. BOP facilities (including contract facilities) were not located in the states that contained large tribal populations and had committed a large number of Indian country juveniles (South Dakota, North Dakota, Montana, and New Mexico). For example, tribal youth whose legal residence was South Dakota comprised over half of the juveniles in BOP facilities in Minnesota.

Among tribal youth under BOP jurisdiction in 2003, most were committed for a violent felony offense, including homicide, manslaughter, serious sexual assault or abuse, and serious physical assault. In comparison, 185 tribal juveniles were in custody in 10 juvenile tribal facilities in 2002. (See *American Indians and Crime*, BJS Web, December 2004.) These tribal youth were confined mostly for misdemeanor (62%) and status offenses (29%); 10% of the youth were confined in tribal juvenile facilities for felony offenses.

### *Tribal Youth Served a Sentence in Federal Facilities that Was Twice as Long as the Maximum Sentence Tribal Facilities Can Impose*

From 1999 to 2008, the average time served by tribal youth tended to be longer (about 26 months, on average) than the tribal justice system maximum sentence of 12 months. The Tribal Law and Order Act of 2010 recently extended the maximum a tribal court can sentence to 3 years for those courts meeting conditions placed on the legal process. The average time served by non-tribal youth in BOP facilities more than doubled from 15 months in 1999 to over 38 months by 2008.

### *Non-Tribal Youth Admitted to the Federal Prison Authorities Were Somewhat More Dispersed than Tribal Youth with Respect to District of Commitment*

About 32% of non-tribal youth were committed from the five federal districts that committed the most tribal youth. Thirty-six percent of non-tribal youth were committed to the BOP from five federal judicial districts along the U.S.-Mexico border: California-Southern, Arizona, New Mexico, Texas-Western, and Texas-Southern. (figure 5.7).

**Table 5.3. Tribal youth admitted to the jurisdiction of the Federal Bureau of Prisons, 1999–2008**

| | | Year of commitment to BOP jurisdiction | | | | | | | | | |
|---|---|---|---|---|---|---|---|---|---|---|---|
| Commitment offense | Total | 1999 | 2000 | 2001 | 2002 | 2003 | 2004 | 2005 | 2006 | 2007 | 2008 |
| Total | 1,909 | 241 | 252 | 219 | 234 | 212 | 231 | 208 | 164 | 76 | 72 |
| Murder/Negligent manslaughter* | 218 | 31 | 27 | 25 | 18 | 20 | 24 | 26 | 20 | 16 | 11 |
| Assault | 491 | 44 | 65 | 70 | 57 | 52 | 64 | 52 | 49 | 20 | 18 |
| Robbery | 51 | 7 | 5 | 9 | 4 | 7 | 9 | 4 | 3 | 1 | 2 |
| Sexual abuse | 441 | 55 | 52 | 33 | 65 | 46 | 55 | 57 | 40 | 17 | 21 |
| Embezzlement | 1 | 1 | 0 | 0 | 0 | 0 | 0 | 0 | 0 | 0 | 0 |
| Burglary | 442 | 62 | 66 | 59 | 61 | 53 | 43 | 42 | 30 | 12 | 14 |
| Larceny | 56 | 12 | 7 | 5 | 8 | 4 | 4 | 6 | 6 | 2 | 2 |
| Motor vehicle theft | 8 | 2 | 1 | 1 | 0 | 1 | 0 | 1 | 2 | 0 | 0 |
| Arson and explosives | 69 | 2 | 6 | 3 | 5 | 11 | 17 | 9 | 6 | 7 | 3 |
| Other property offenses | 38 | 13 | 6 | 6 | 4 | 1 | 3 | 3 | 1 | 1 | 0 |
| Other drug felonies | 3 | 0 | 1 | 0 | 0 | 1 | 0 | 1 | 0 | 0 | 0 |
| Weapon offenses | 9 | 1 | 2 | 0 | 2 | 1 | 2 | 1 | 0 | 0 | 0 |
| Nonviolent sex offenses | 36 | 4 | 4 | 1 | 4 | 7 | 7 | 3 | 5 | 0 | 1 |
| Traffic offenses | 13 | 2 | 5 | 1 | 1 | 3 | 1 | 0 | 0 | 0 | 0 |

Note: Total includes juveniles whose offenses were missing or unclassifiable.

*Includes attempted murder.

Source: Urban Institute analysis of Federal Bureau of Prisons, SENTRY data base, fiscal years 1999-2008.

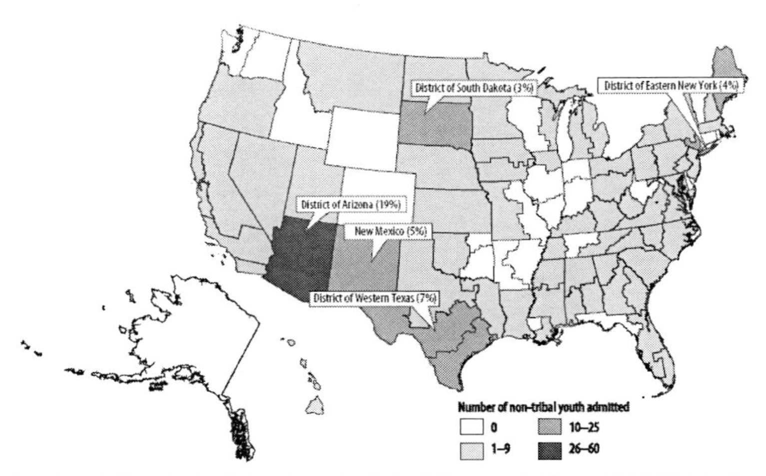


Source: Based on BJS analysis of data from the Federal Bureau of Prisons, SENTRY database, fiscal years 2006–2008.

Figure 5.7. Non-tribal youth admitted to the jurisdiction of the Federal Bureau of Prisons, and five federal judicial districts that committed the majority of non-tribal youth, 2006–2008.

### *Among Juveniles Admitted to the Jurisdiction of the BOP in 2008, Non-Tribal Youth Were Slightly Older at Age of Offense than Tribal Youth*

The average of age tribal youth at time of offense was about 15 years compared to 16 years for non-tribal youth. Most tribal youth were male (92%), American Indian (96%), non-Hispanic (99%), and United States citizens (100%). The majority of non-tribal youth were male (93%), white (60%), non-Hispanic (58%), and United States citizens (71%).

## Methodology

The primary source of data presented in this report is from the Federal Justice Statistics Program (FJSP). The methodology to identify tribal youth was developed by the Urban Institute, and primary findings reported here are drawn from their 2011 study, *Tribal Youth in the Federal Justice System* (http://ncjrs.gov). This report supplemented findings from the Urban Institute's study with additional analyses based on BJS analysis of FJSP data. Data from the Federal Bureau of Prisons (BOP), SENTRY database, which contains information on all federally sentenced offenders admitted to BOP jurisdiction at fiscal yearend were analyzed for the years 1994 to 1998.

The source of the data in figure 5.1 is The Urban Institute analysis of Executive Office for U.S. Attorneys, National LIONS database, fiscal years 2000 to 2008. Suspects in matters concluded include all matters which were concluded in each respective year. Suspects in matters prosecuted include matters for which the U.S. attorneys in that district made the decision to prosecute the matter in each fiscal year. The unit of count for figure 5.1 is the suspect matter.

A matter is a referral on which an attorney spends one hour or more investigating, and on which formal papers have not been filed with the Court. If a decision is made not to continue with the investigation, it is disposed of in the LIONS database by declination and closed.

## References

*American Indians and Crime*, NCJ 203097, BJS Web, December 2004.

*2005 American Indian Population and Labor Force Report*. U.S. Department of the Interior, Bureau of Indian Affairs, 2005.

The Urban Institute. *Tribal Youth in the Federal Justice System*, NCJ 234549, May 2011. Available at http://ncjrs.gov.

Researchers from The Urban Institute investigated how youth from Indian Country were processed by the federal criminal justice system. They used a combination of qualitative and quantitative information, including administrative data from the BJS-sponsored Federal Justice Statistics Program (FJSP) and information drawn from interviews with more than three dozen federal and tribal justice system personnel.

Staff at the Urban Institute who contributed to the study included—

Co-principal Investigators
William Adams and Julie Samuels
Contextual Analysis Team
Janeen Buck Willison, Hannah Dodd, and Meredith Dank
Quantitative Analysis Team
Barbara Parthasarathy, Kamala Mallik Kane, Jessica Kelly, Sybil Mendonca, and KiDeuk Kim

In: Criminal Justice in Indian Country
Editors: D. Mercato and E. Rojas ISBN: 978-1-62100-267-3


*Chapter 2*

# JAILS IN INDIAN COUNTRY, 2009*

## *United States Department of Justice*

Todd D. Minton
BJS Statistician

At midyear 2009, a total of 2,176 inmates were confined in Indian country jails, a 1.9% increase from the 2,135 inmates confined at midyear 2008 (figure 1). This count was based on data from 80 facilities, including jails, confinement facilities, detention centers, and other correctional facilities, that were in operation in Indian country at midyear 2009. For 2008, the number of inmates was based on data for 82 facilities in operation at midyear 2008. The number of inmates held in Indian country jails between 2004 and 2009 increased by 25% from 1,745 to 2,176. On June 30, 2009, the number of American Indians and Alaska Natives confined in jails outside of Indian country (9,400) was more than 4 times the number held in jails in Indian country.

---

* This is an edited, reformatted and augmented version of the United States Department of Justice publication, NCJ 232223, dated on February 2011.

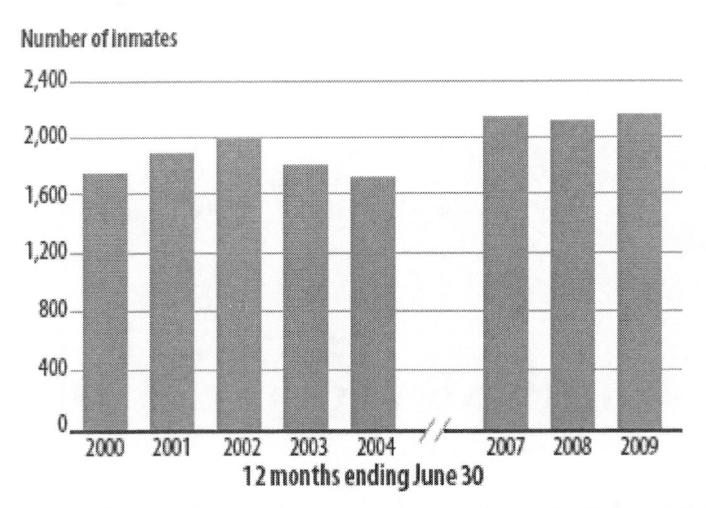


Note: The Survey of Jails in Indian Country was not conducted in 2005 and 2006.

Figure 1. Inmates confined in Indian country jails, 2000-2004 and 2007-2009.

## The Number of Jails in Indian Country Has Increased between 2004 and 2009

The Bureau of Justice Statistics (BJS) collected data from 68 correctional facilities in Indian country in 2004, from 79 in 2007, from 82 in 2008, and from 80 in 2009. The survey was not conducted in 2005 and 2006. Over the 5-year period, a number of facilities closed and new facilities became operational. Eleven facilities permanently closed between 2004 and 2009 and a total of 21 facilities were newly constructed. BJS estimated inmate population counts for 7 facilities in 2004 and 4 facilities in 2007 that did not respond to the surveys. All known operating facilities responded to the 2008 and 2009 surveys. See *Methodology* for additional details on facility counts and participation in the surveys.

## Highlights

- The number of inmates confined in Indian country jails increased by 1.9% between midyear 2008 and 2009, reaching 2,176 inmates.

- Nationwide, American Indians and Alaska Natives under correctional supervision in the U.S. increased 5.6 percent, from an estimated 75,400 offenders in 2008 to 79,600 in 2009. Nearly two-thirds of the population (63 percent or 50,200) was under supervision in the community on probation or parole in 2009, and about a third (29,400 or 37 percent) was in prison or jail.
- Over the 12 months ending June 2009, the average daily jail population in Indian country increased by 12%, and the percentage of occupied bed space increased from 64.2% to 73.5%.
- Eleven jails (14% of all facilities) held 51% of inmates confined at midyear 2009.
- During June 2009, the number of inmates admitted into Indian country jails (11,357) was about 5 times the size of the average daily population (2,124).
- The expected average length of stay increased by a half day from 5.1 days during June 2008 to 5.6 days during June 2009.
- Indian country jail authorities reported no deaths in custody between July 1, 2008, and June 30, 2009, down from 4 reported deaths during the 12-month period ending June 30, 2008; attempted suicides by inmates declined from 78 in 2008 to 56 in 2009.
- Indian country jails held fewer inmates for domestic violence at midyear 2009 (252), continuing the downward trend in the number held for this offense since 2007 (362).
- The percentage of certified correctional officers working in Indian country jails increased steadily, from 63% at midyear 2007 to 79% at midyear 2009.

## American Indian and Alaska Natives Under Correctional Supervision

*The number of American Indians and Alaska Natives on probation or parole, or incarcerated in jail or prison reached 79,600 at midyear 2009, up nearly 6% from midyear 2008 and 12% from midyear 2007.*

According to the U.S. Census Bureau's National Population Estimates, 3,151,284 American Indians and Alaska Natives lived in the United States on July 1, 2009, accounting for about 1% of the U.S. resident population.

The number of American Indians and Alaska Natives in jail or prison accounted for 1.3% (29,400) of all inmates in custody in jail or prison in the U.S. The local governing authority on Indian lands is typically a tribal government or council. Jurisdiction over crimes in Indian country depends on several factors, including the identity of the victim and the offender, the severity of the crime, and the location where the crime was committed. Tribal jurisdiction includes crimes committed by Indians in Indian country. Tribal rights to sentence offenders are limited to 1 year of imprisonment, a $5,000 fine, or both (25 U.S.C. § 1302(7)). Federal jurisdiction over crime in Indian country includes 14 crimes under the Major Crimes Act of 1885 (18 U.S.C. § 1153), and state jurisdiction includes all crimes on tribal lands specified under Public Law 280 (18 U.S.C. § 1162).

At midyear 2009, tribal, federal, state, and local jail correctional authorities held 932 American Indians per 100,000 American Indian U.S. residents. (American Indians in this report include Alaska Natives.) The incarceration rate for American Indians was about 25% higher than the overall national incarceration rate of 747 per 100,000 persons other than American Indians or Alaska Natives. Federal, state, local, and tribal correctional authorities supervised an estimated 79,600 American Indians in 2009, up from 75,400 in 2008 (figure 2). Between 2000 and 2009, the number of American Indians confined in jails and prisons nationwide grew on average by about 4.3% annually.

Among American Indians under any form of correctional supervision in 2009, most (63% or 50,200) were supervised in the community on probation or parole (table 1). A total of 29,400 American Indians were in jail or prison at midyear 2009. Almost 50% (14,646) were held in state prison, and about 11% were held in federal prison (3,154). The remaining 11,576 American Indians were confined in Indian country jails (2,176) and local jails (9,400). Some American Indians confined in local jails may have been adjudicated by a tribal criminal justice system and housed in jails under contracts with tribal, city, or county governments.

Between midyear 2008 and 2009, the number of American Indians under correctional supervision increased by 5.6%. The number of American Indians confined in jails and prisons nationwide grew by approximately 3.5% from 2008 to 2009. Over the 12-month period, the largest growth in the confined American Indian population occurred in federal prison (5.5%) followed by local jails (4.4%), state prisons (2.7%), and Indian country jails (1.9%).

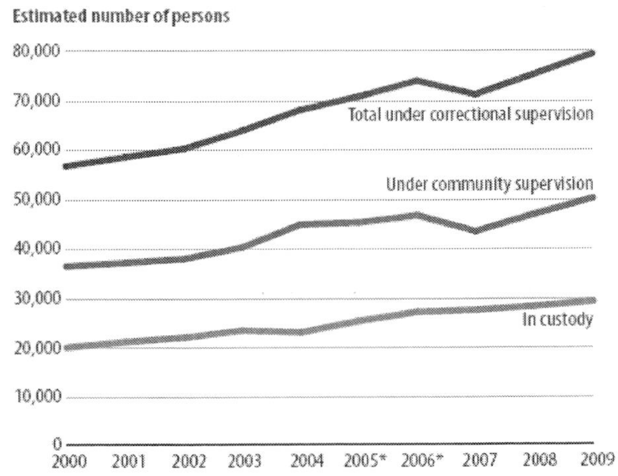


Note: Indian country jail populations were estimated for 2005 and 2006 based on the average annual population change for jails reporting in both 2004 and 2007.

Figure 2. American Indians and Alaska Natives under correctional supervision in the United States, 2000-2009.

## Table 1. American Indians and Alaska Natives in custody or under community supervision, 2008 and 2009

| | Number | | Percent change |
|---|---|---|---|
| | 2008 | 2009 | |
| Total | 75,400 | 79,600 | 5.6% |
| In custody at midyear | 28,400 | 29,400 | 3.5% |
| Local jails[a] | 9,000 | 9,400 | 4.4 |
| Jails in Indian country | 2,135 | 2,176 | 1.9 |
| State prisons | 14,264 | 14,646 | 2.7 |
| Federal prisons | 2,989 | 3,154 | 5.5 |
| Under community supervision[b] | 47,000 | 50,200 | 6.8% |
| State/federal | | | |
| Probation | 39,100 | 41,600 | 6.4 |
| Parole | 7,900 | 8,600 | 8.9 |

Note: Detail may not sum to total because of rounding.

[a] Estimated from the Annual Survey of Jails. See *Jail Inmates at Midyear 2008-Statistical Tables* and *Jail Inmates at Midyear 2009-Statistical Tables* for estimated standard errors.

[b] Probation and parole counts are based on yearend 2007 and 2008; counts were estimated by applying the percent of probation and parole population with known characteristics to the total number of probationers and parolees.

## On an Average Day in June, the Percentage of Occupied Bed Space Increased from 64.2% to 73.5%

At midyear 2009, the 80 jail facilities in Indian country were rated to hold 2,891 inmates, down from 2,963 in 82 facilities during the same period in 2008 (table 2). The average daily population (ADP) in June—the population measure used to calculate percent of capacity occupied— increased by nearly 12%, from 1,903 (June 2008) to 2,124 inmates (June 2009), while the capacity to hold inmates decreased by 2%. Consequently, the percentage of rated capacity occupied in Indian country jails increased from 64% to 73% during the 12-month period. On June 30, 2009, the 80 facilities held a total of 2,176 inmates and were operating at 75% of rated capacity, remaining relatively stable since 2007. From June 2004 to June 2009, the overall number of beds (or rated capacity) grew at a faster rate (34%) than the the inmate population (25%).

## About 9 in 10 Inmates Were Confined in the Larger Indian Country Jails Rated to Hold 25 or More Inmates

Of the 2,176 inmates confined in 80 Indian country jails at midyear 2009, about 87% (1,884) were held in 45 facilities rated to hold 25 or more inmates (table 3). Nearly equal shares of inmates were held in 30 facilities rated to hold 25 to 49 inmates (42%) and in 15 facilities rated to hold 50 or more inmates (44%). The 35 facilities with a rated capacity of fewer than 25 inmates accounted for about 44% of all facilities and held about 13% of all jail inmates in Indian country.

At midyear 2009, Indian country jails held an average of 27 inmates per facility. The confined jail population ranged from a low of no inmates in 7 facilities to a high of 192 inmates in the Tohono O'odham Adult Detention Center. This facility held nearly 9% of the total population in Indian country jails at midyear 2009.

Eleven jails held more than half (51%) of the total inmate population at midyear 2009 (table 4). Between midyear 2008 and midyear 2009, the population in these jails increased by 247 inmates (29%). In 2008, 9 of the 11 facilities held the majority of jail inmates in Indian country.

Over the 365-day period, 6 jails that held the majority of inmates in Indian country in 2008 experienced large declines in their jail populations. The combined decrease in the size of the jail population in these facilities was 33% (90 inmates) from midyear 2008 to midyear 2009.

**Table 2. Inmates, rated capacity, and percent of capacity occupied in Indian country jails, 2004 and 2007-2009**

| | 2004 | 2007 | 2008 | 2009 |
|---|---|---|---|---|
| Number of inmates | | | | |
| Midyear | 1,745 | 2,163 | 2,135 | 2,176 |
| ADPa | 1,622 | 2,046 | 1,903 | 2,124 |
| Rated capacity | 2,162 | 2,900 | 2,963 | 2,891 |
| Percent of capacity occupiedb | | | | |
| Midyear | 80.7% | 74.6% | 72.1% | 75.3% |
| ADP | 75.0 | 70.6 | 64.2 | 73.5 |
| Number of operating facilities | 68 | 79 | 82 | 80 |

[a] Average daily population is the number of inmates confined each day in June divided by 30.

[b] The average daily population was divided by rated capacity (maximum number of beds or inmates assigned by a rating official) multiplied by 100 percent.

**Table 3. Indian country jails and percent of inmate population, by facility size, June 2009**

| | Number | | Percent | |
|---|---|---|---|---|
| Facility size* | Facilities | Inmates | Facilities | Inmates |
| Total | 80 | 2,176 | 100% | 100% |
| Fewer than 10 inmates | 11 | 12 | 13.8% | 0.6% |
| 10 to 24 | 24 | 280 | 30.0 | 12.9 |
| 25 to 49 | 30 | 920 | 37.5 | 42.3 |
| 50 or more | 15 | 964 | 18.8 | 44.3 |

Note: Detail may not sum to total because of rounding.

*Based on the rated capacity, maximum number of beds or inmates assigned by a rating official.

Among the 11 facilities holding the majority of inmates in 2009, the Gila River Department of Corrections and Supervision-Adult facility reported the largest decline (30 inmates or 17%) in the number of jail inmates. The jail population in this facility has decreased by 92 inmates (38%) from its peak of 241 inmates reported at midyear 2007.

Two facilities, the Truxton Canyon Adult Detention Center and the Laguna Tribal Police and Detention Center, were among the 11 facilities holding the majority of jail inmates in 2009. These two facilities were not among the 11 facilities holding the majority of inmates in 2008 (See *Jails in Indian Country, 2008*, NCJ 228271, BJS website, December 2008).

The Truxton Canyon Adult Detention Center reported the largest increase in the inmate population (66 inmates or 169%) between midyear 2008 and midyear 2009. The Laguna Tribal Police and Detention Center increased by 58% (19 inmates) between 2008 and 2009.

Based on the 80 facilities responding to the survey in both 2008 and 2009, the overall change in the inmate population (up 45 inmates) was relatively small. Thirty-three facilities, mostly the larger facilities, accounted for this increase (not shown in table).

Change in the size of the jail population in Indian country was varied. More than half of the 80 jails experienced either a decline (40 jails) or no change (7 jails) in the size of their inmate population over the 12-month period ending midyear 2009. Overall, the 50% increase (415 inmates) in the jail population in 33 jails was offset by a 30% decline (370 inmates) in 40 jails.

## The Use of Jail Space Varied by Facility Size

Indian country jails rated to hold 25 to 49 inmates were operating at 89% of their rated capacity on June 30, 2009, and at 79% on an average day in June. An average day in June was based on the average daily population, or the sum of the numbers held on each day in June, divided by 30. In contrast, the lowest percentage of capacity occupied during June 2009 was among the 11 small jails rated to hold fewer than 10 inmates. These facilities were operating at 21% of rated capacity at midyear and at 17% of capacity on an average day in June 2009 (figure 3).

Compared to facilities in all other size categories, the large jails with a rated capacity of 50 or more inmates reported the only increase in occupied bed space between 2008 and 2009. The percentage of capacity occupied in these jails increased from 51% to 69% during the 12 months ending at midyear 2009, and from 49% to 73% on an average day in June 2008 and 2009.

**Table 4. Jails in Indian country that held the majority of inmates, by facility, June 2009**

| Facility | Custody population at midyear | | Change in population | |
|---|---|---|---|---|
| | 2008 | 2009 | Number | Percent |
| Total, 11 facilities | 859 | 1,106 | 247 | 29% |
| Tohono O'odham Adult Detention Center (AZ) | 137 | 192 | 55 | 40% |
| Gila River Department of Rehabilitation and Supervision - Adult (AZ) | 179 | 149 | -30 | -17 |
| San Carlos Department of Corrections and Rehabilitation - Adult and Juvenile Detention (AZ) | 88 | 147 | 59 | 67 |
| Truxton Canyon Adult Detention Center (AZ) | 39 | 105 | 66 | 169 |
| White Mountain Apache Detention Center (AZ) | 101 | 95 | -6 | -6 |
| Oglala Sioux Tribal Offenders Facility (SD) | 52 | 95 | 43 | 83 |
| Standing Rock Law Enforcement and Adult Detention Center (ND) | 71 | 93 | 22 | 31 |
| Nisqually Adult Corrections (WA) | 59 | 73 | 14 | 24 |
| Menominee Tribal Detention Facility (WI) | 54 | 53 | -1 | -2 |
| Navajo Department of Corrections - Shiprock Police Department and Adult Detention (NM) | 46 | 52 | 6 | 13 |
| Laguna Tribal Police and Detention Center (NM) | 33 | 52 | 19 | 58 |

The amount of bed space occupied was also measured based on a facility's most crowded day in June. Nearly half (38 facilities) of the 80 facilities in Indian country were operating above rated capacity on the most crowded day in June (table 5). Of those facilities, 18 were operating above rated capacity on June 30, and 13 were operating above rated capacity on an average day during June 2009.

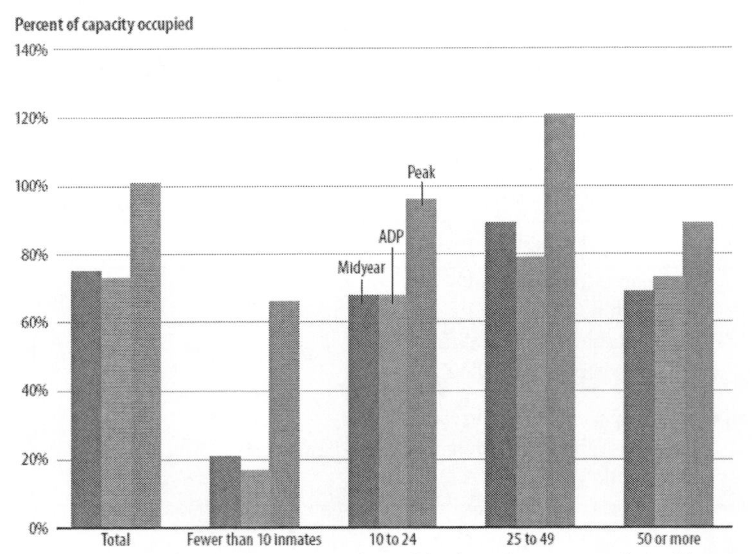


Note: Rated capacity is the maximum number of beds or inmates assigned by a rating official. Midyear count is the number of inmates held on the last weekday in June. Average daily population (ADP) is the number of inmates confined in June divided by 30. Peak population is the population held on the day in June in which the custody population of a facility was the largest.

Figure 3. Percent of rated capacity occupied, by type of inmate count, June 2009.

## Thirteen Jails Were Operating at More than 50% over Capacity on Their Most Crowded Day in June 2009

At midyear 2009, 13 jails in Indian country reported operating at more than 50% over rated capacity on the facility's most crowded day in June 2009, down from 18 facilities during June 2008 (table 6). Eight of these 13 jails were rated to hold 25 or more inmates, and 5 were rated to hold fewer than 25 inmates.

Tohono O'odham Adult Detention Center (AZ), with a rated capacity of 107 inmates, was the largest of these jails and operated at 86% over capacity on its peak day in June 2009. Between July 2008 and June 2009, this facility was renovated to accommodate 73 additional beds. As a result, the percent of occupied space declined from 429% on the facility's most crowded day in June 2008 to 186% in June 2009.

**Table 5. Number of Indian country jails, by percent of rated capacity occupied, June 2009**

| | Number of jails | | |
|---|---|---|---|
| Percent of capacity occupied[a] | Midyear | ADP[b] | Peak[c] |
| Less than 25% | 17 | 20 | 7 |
| 25-49% | 15 | 11 | 8 |
| 50-74% | 19 | 21 | 15 |
| 75-100% | 11 | 15 | 12 |
| More than 100% | 18 | 13 | 38 |

[a] Population as a percent of capacity occupied is calculated by dividing the population count of a facility by its rated capacity and multiplying by 100.
[b] Average daily population (ADP) is the sum of the number of inmates held on each day in June, divided by 30.
[c] Peak population is the population held on the day in June in which the custody population of a facility was the largest.

Among the 13 facilities operating at more than 50% over rated capacity on their most crowded day in June, 7 were also operating at more than 50% over capacity at midyear 2009 and 5 on an average day in June 2009. Four facilities were operating at more than 50% over capacity on all three measures (midyear, most crowed day, and the average day in June 2009): White Mountain Apache Detention Center, Truxton Canyon Adult Detention Center, Northern Cheyenne Adult Detention Center, and the Tohono O'odham Adult Detention Center.

## High Volumes of Admissions of Inmates Were Processed through Indian Country Jails

Eighty Indian country jails admitted 11,357 persons during June 2009, up slightly from 11,149 admissions in 81 facilities during June 2008 (table 7). The number of admissions grew by 1.6% in the 79 facilities that reported data on admissions in both June 2009 (11,323) and June 2008 (11,147) (not shown in a table).

**Table 6. Jails in Indian country operating above 150% of capacity on their peak day, during June 2009**

| Facilities operating above capacity | Peak population in June[a] | Rated capacity[b] | Percent of capacity occupied on peak day in June | Number of inmates over capacity |
|---|---|---|---|---|
| Total, 13 facilities | 1,017 | 525 | : | : |
| White Mountain Apache Detention Center (AZ) | 139 | 45 | 309% | 94 |
| San Juan Pueblo Police Department Holding Facility (NM) | 6 | 2 | 300 | 4 |
| Truxton Canyon Adult Detention Center (AZ) | 105 | 40 | 263 | 65 |
| Cheyenne River Sioux Juvenile Detention Center (SD) | 23 | 10 | 230 | 13 |
| Northern Cheyenne Adult Detention Center (MT) | 43 | 19 | 226 | 24 |
| Tohono O'odham Adult Detention Center (AZ) | 199 | 107 | 186 | 92 |
| Kyle Police Department and Adult Detention (SD) | 44 | 24 | 183 | 20 |
| Standing Rock Law Enforcement and Adult Detention Center (ND) | 86 | 48 | 179 | 38 |
| Navajo Department of Corrections - Window Rock (AZ) | 75 | 42 | 179 | 33 |
| Fort Peck Police Department and Adult Detention Center (MT) | 39 | 22 | 177 | 17 |
| Fort Totten Law Enforcement and Adult Detention Center (ND) | 42 | 26 | 162 | 16 |
| Gila River Department of Rehabilitation and Supervision - Adult (AZ) | 164 | 106 | 155 | 58 |
| Navajo Department of Corrections - Shiprock Police Department and Adult Detention (NM) | 52 | 34 | 153 | 18 |

Note: See table 10 for a list of all facilities and the capacity occupied.

:Not calculated.

[a] Peak population is the population held on the day in June in which the custody population of a facility was the largest.

[b] Rated capacity is the maximum number of beds or inmates assigned by a rating official.

Admissions to facilities rated to hold between 25 to 49 inmates accounted for about 48% (5,503) of all admissions in June 2009, down from 59% of all admissions in June 2008. The largest Indian country jails accounted for less than 20% of all facilities and reported a total increase of nearly 75% in the number of jail admissions during the 12-month period. Admissions to the largest Indian country jails increased from 1,915 to 3,342 from June 2008 to June 2009. The 15 jails rated to hold 50 or more inmates had the highest average number of admissions per month (233), compared to jails in all other size categories (not shown).

## Inmate Deaths and Attempted Suicides in Indian Country Jails Declined

Indian country jail authorities reported no deaths in custody between July 1, 2008, and June 30, 2009, down from 4 reported deaths during the 12-month period ending June 30, 2008. Attempted suicides by inmates declined from 78 in 2008 to 56 in 2009.

## Expected Length of Stay Was 5.6 Days for Indian Country Jail Inmates in June 2009

During June 2009, the expected average length of stay for inmates confined in Indian country jails was 5.6 days, up from 5.1 days during June 2008. Length of stay is the time held in custody from admission to release. The expected length of stay for inmates was the highest (9.1 days) in facilities that were rated to hold 50 or more inmates, down from 10.3 days in June 2008. Inmates held in jails rated to hold less than 10 inmates experienced the shortest expected length of stay (2.1 days).

## Inmate Characteristics Remain Relatively Unchanged; The Number Held for Domestic Violence Declined

Inmate characteristics by sex, age, and offense have changed in absolute numbers since 2000 (table 8). However, the distribution within most categories remained stable between 2000 and 2008, with a change in the distribution of inmates by sex, conviction status, and offense type at midyear 2009.

**Table 7. Admissions and expected length of stay in Indian country jails during June, by facility size, June 2009**

| Facility size[a] | Number of facilities | ADP[b] | Estimated June admissions | Expected average length of stay[c] |
|---|---|---|---|---|
| Total | 80 | 2,124 | 11,357 | 5.6 days |
| Fewer than 10 inmates | 11 | 9 | 133 | 2.1 |
| 10 to 24 | 24 | 276 | 2,379 | 3.5 |
| 25 to 49 | 30 | 820 | 5,503 | 4.5 |
| 50 or more | 15 | 1,018 | 3,342 | 9.1 |

[a] Based on the rated capacity, the maximum number of beds or inmates assigned by a rating official.

[b] Detail may not sum to total due to rounding.

[c] Expected length of stay was calculated by dividing the average daily population (ADP) by the number of June admissions, and multiplying by 30. See *Methodology* for details on estimating expected length of stay.

Adult males have accounted for the largest portion of the inmate population in Indian country jails during the decade. The female jail population has had small but steady increases from midyear 2000 to 2008, with a nearly 8% decrease in the size of this population between midyear 2008 and midyear 2009. Except for one juvenile female inmate, the decline was entirely among the adult female jail population.

The percentage of convicted inmates increased from 57% in 2002 to 69% in 2009. Inmates confined for a violent offense made up about 37% of the jail population at midyear 2009, down from 41% at midyear 2008. Most (75%) of this decline was among the population held for domestic violence. Domestic violence (12%) and simple or aggravated assault (15%) accounted for the largest percentage of violent offenders held in 2009, followed by unspecified violent offenses (8%) and rape or sexual assault (2%). Since peaking at midyear 2007, the percentage of inmates held for domestic violence has steadily declined, from 20% in 2007 to 12% in 2009. The Gila River Department of Corrections-Adult accounted for a large portion of the decline in domestic violence offenders between 2007 and 2009. It reported a 38% decrease in the confined inmate population between midyear 2007 (241) and midyear 2009 (149), and a 74% decline in the number of inmates held for a domestic violence (from 180 in 2007 to 46 in 2009).

**by demographic, characteristics, and offense, June 2000-June 2009**

| Characteristic | Number of inmates | | | | | | Percent of inmates | | | | | |
|---|---|---|---|---|---|---|---|---|---|---|---|---|
| | 2000 | 2002 | 2004 | 2007 | 2008 | 2009 | 2000 | 2002 | 2004 | 2007 | 2008 | 2009 |
| Total | 1,775 | 2,006 | 1,745 | 1,996 | 2,135 | 2,176 | 100% | 100% | 100% | 100% | 100% | 100% |
| Sex | | | | | | | | | | | | |
| Male | 1,421 | 1,618 | 1,346 | 1,582 | 1,678 | 1,754 | 80% | 81% | 77% | 79% | 79% | 81% |
| Female | 354 | 388 | 398 | 414 | 457 | 422 | 20 | 19 | 23 | 21 | 21 | 19 |
| Age group/sex Adults | 1,498 | 1,699 | 1,546 | 1,743 | 1,882 | 1,919 | 84% | 85% | 89% | 87% | 88% | 88% |
| Male | 1,214 | 1,399 | 1,222 | 1,415 | 1,498 | 1,571 | 68 | 70 | 70 | 71 | 70 | 72 |
| Female | 284 | 300 | 324 | 328 | 384 | 348 | 16 | 15 | 19 | 16 | 18 | 16 |
| Juveniles | 277 | 307 | 198 | 253 | 253 | 257 | 16 | 15 | 11 | 13 | 12 | 12 |
| Male | 207 | 219 | 124 | 167 | 180 | 183 | 12 | 11 | 7 | 8 | 8 | 8 |
| Female | 70 | 88 | 74 | 86 | 73 | 74 | 4 | 4 | 4 | 4 | 3 | 3 |

**Table 8. (Continued)**

| Characteristic | Number of inmates | | | | | | Percent of inmates | | | | | |
|---|---|---|---|---|---|---|---|---|---|---|---|---|
| | 2000 | 2002 | 2004 | 2007 | 2008 | 2009 | 2000 | 2002 | 2004 | 2007 | 2008 | 2009 |
| Conviction status | | | | | | | | | | | | |
| Convicted | 1,072 | 1,120 | 966 | 1,116 | 1,340 | 1,496 | 61% | 57% | 58% | 59% | 63% | 69% |
| Unconvicted | 689 | 857 | 697 | 763 | 776 | 680 | 39 | 43 | 42 | 41 | 37 | 31 |
| Type of offense | | | | | | | | | | | | |
| Domestic violence | ... | 291 | 257 | 362 | 307 | 252 | ...% | 15% | 18% | 20% | 15% | 12% |
| Assault | ... | ... | 190 | 233 | 308 | 299 | ... | ... | 13 | 13 | 15 | 15 |
| Rape or sexual assault | ... | ... | 34 | 45 | 42 | 42 | ... | ... | 2 | 2 | 2 | 2 |
| Other violence | ... | ... | 79 | 108 | 177 | 168 | ... | ... | 6 | 6 | 9 | 8 |
| DWI/DUI* | 274 | 226 | 195 | 137 | 184 | 229 | 17 | 11 | 14 | 8 | 9 | 11 |
| Drug law violation | 133 | 126 | 104 | 132 | 104 | 107 | 8 | 6 | 7 | 7 | 5 | 5 |
| Other | ... | ... | 569 | 804 | 954 | 955 | ... | ... | 40 | 44 | 46 | 47 |
| Offense not reported | ... | ... | 317 | 175 | 59 | 124 | / | / | / | / | / | / |

Note: Detailed characteristics may not be equal to the total number of confined inmates because of incomplete data. See appendix tables 1-3 for a list of all facilities and inmate characteristics. *Includes driving while intoxicated and driving while under the influence of drugs or alcohol.

...Not collected.

/Not reported.

## Steady Increase in the Number of Certified Correctional Officers and in-Service Training

Seventy-nine Indian country jails employed 1,332 persons at midyear 2009 (table 9). About 69% (916) of all personnel were jail operations staff, including correctional officers and other staff who spent more than 50% of their time supervising inmates. The remaining 416 jail personnel included administrative employees, educational staff, technical or professional staff, clerical, maintenance, or food service staff, and other job functions. Overall, the ratio of inmates to jail operations employees was 2.4 inmates to 1 em-ployee at midyear 2009, remaining relatively stable since 2008 (2.3 to 1) and 2004 (2.5 to 1). Seventy-six facilities reported that 710 (79%) correctional officers had received basic detention officer certification, up from 69% in 2008 and 63% in 2007 (not shown). Seventy-four facilities reported that 750 (84%) correctional officers had received 40 hours of in-service training, up from 74% in 2008 and 70% in 2007.

**Table 9. Number of persons employed in Indian country jails, by job function, June 2009**

| Job functions | Number | Percent |
|---|---|---|
| Total[a] | 1,332 | 100% |
| Administrative[b] | 136 | 10.2% |
| Jail operations | 916 | 68.8 |
| Educational staff | 29 | 2.2 |
| Technical/professional | 51 | 3.8 |
| Clerical/maintenance/food service | 173 | 13.0 |
| Number of inmates per jail operations staff | 2.4 | |

[a] Includes 27 other unspecified functions not shown in table.

[b] Includes jail administrators, assistants, and other personnel who work in an administrative capacity more than 50% of the time.

## Methodology

The Annual Survey of Jails in Indian Country (SJIC) includes all known Indian country correctional facilities operated by tribal authorities or the Bureau of Indian Affairs (BIA), U.S. Department of the Interior. The survey was conducted in June 2009 and included the number of inmates and percent of capacity occupied based on the ADP, midyear population, and peak population in facilities in June 2009 (table 10).

Through a cooperative agreement with BJS, Westat, Inc. conducted the SJIC to describe all adult and juvenile jail facilities and detention centers in Indian country. For this report, Indian country includes reservations, pueblos, rancherias, and other appropriate areas (18 U.S.C.§ 1151). The reference date for the survey is June 30, 2009.

Annually, BIA provides BJS a list of Indian country jail facilities, including detention centers, jails, and other correctional facilities operated by tribal authorities or BIA. BJS uses this list to update its existing roster of jails in Indian country. BJS obtains data from administrators of Indian country jails by mailed questionnaires and through follow-up phone calls and facsimiles.

In 2004, BJS contacted administrators in 70 facilities to participate in the survey. BJS received responses from 61 facilities; 7 did not respond, and 2 facilities were non-operational. In 2007, the BJS roster consisted of 86 facilities. Seventy-nine of the facility administrators responded to the survey; 4 did not respond, and BJS found that 3 facilities were non-operational. In 2008, BJS's roster of Indian country jails consisted of 85 facilities. BJS received responses from 82 facility administrators; there were no nonrespondents, and 3 facilities were non-operational. For 2009, the BJS roster consisted of 86 facilities. BJS received responses from 80 facility administrators; there were no nonrespondents, and 6 facilities were non-operational. For comparison over time, BJS estimated data on inmate populations for the 7 facilities in 2004 and 4 facilities in 2008 that did not respond to the surveys.

### *Expected Length of Stay*

The stock-flow ratio method was used to measure the expected average length of stay for inmates held during June 2009 in the 80 Indian country jails that responded to stock and flow items in the survey:

Stock—average daily population

Flow—inmate admissions during June 2009

Stock-flow ratio in June 2009

(2,124/11,357=0.187)

Expected length of stay in days (0.187 × 30)—is the average number of days held in custody from admission to release.

*Indian country* is a statutory term that includes all lands within an Indian reservation, dependent Indian communities, and Indian trust allotments (18 U.S.C. § 1151). Courts interpret Section 1151 to include all lands held in trust for tribes or their members. (See United States v. Roberts, 185 F.3d 1125 (10th Cir. 1999).) Tribal authority to imprison American Indian offenders is limited to one year per offense by statute (25 U.S.C. § 1302), a $5,000 fine, or both.

Tribal law enforcement agencies act as first responders to both felony and misdemeanor crimes. For most of Indian country, the federal government provides felony law enforcement concerning crimes by or against Indians. Certain areas of Indian country are under Public Law 83-280, as amended. P.L. 280 conferred jurisdiction on certain states over Indian country and suspended enforcement of the Major Crimes Act (18 U.S.C. § 1153) and the General Crimes Act (18 U.S.C. § 1152) in those areas. Indian tribes retain concurrent jurisdiction to enforce laws in Indian country where P.L. 280 applies.

**occupied in Indian country, by facility, June 2009**

| | Number of inmates | | | | Percent of capacity[a] | | |
|---|---|---|---|---|---|---|---|
| State and facility | Inmates in custody[b] | ADP[c] | Peak population in June[d] | Rated capacity[e] | Population on June 30[a] | ADP[a] | Peak population in June[a] |
| Total | 2,176 | 2,124 | : | 2,891 | 75% | 73% | : |
| Alaska | | | | | | | |
| Metlakatla Juvenile Detention Center | 0 | 0 | 0 | 0 | 0% | 0% | 0% |
| Metlakatla Police Department and Adult Detention Center | 0 | 1 | 5 | 5 | 0 | 20 | 100 |
| Arizona | | | | | | | |
| Ak-Chin Tribal Police and Detention Center | 11 | 31 | 13 | 22 | 50% | 141% | 59% |
| Colorado River Indian Tribes Adult Detention Center | 37 | 33 | 38 | 36 | 103 | 92 | 106 |
| Fort McDowell Police Department and Holding Facility | 8 | 5 | 8 | 10 | 80 | 50 | 80 |
| Fort Mohave Tribal Police Department and Holding Facility | 1 | 0 | 3 | 6 | 17 | 0 | 50 |
| Gila River Department of Rehabilitation and Supervision - Adult | 149 | 162 | 164 | 106 | 141 | 153 | 155 |
| Gila River Department of Rehabilitation and Supervision - Juvenile | 30 | 25 | 34 | 106 | 28 | 24 | 32 |
| Navajo Department of Corrections - Chinle | 0 | 0 | 0 | 0 | : | : | : |

**Table 10. (Continued)**

| State and facility | Number of inmates | | | Percent of capacity[a] | | | |
|---|---|---|---|---|---|---|---|
| | Inmates in custody[b] | ADP[c] | Peak population in June[d] | Rated capacity[e] | Population on June 30[a] | ADP[a] | Peak population in June[a] |
| Navajo Department of Corrections-Kayenta Police Department and Holding Facility | 11 | 11 | 15 | 10 | 110 | 110 | 150 |
| Navajo Department of Corrections - Tuba City | 17 | 20 | 34 | 32 | 53 | 63 | 106 |
| Navajo Department of Corrections - Window Rock | 34 | 34 | 75 | 42 | 81 | 81 | 179 |
| Pascua Yaqui Police Department and Holding Facility | 1 | 3 | 4 | 8 | 13 | 38 | 50 |
| Salt River Pima-Maricopa Department of Corrections | 25 | 23 | 29 | 186 | 13 | 12 | 16 |
| San Carlos Department of Corrections and Rehabilitation - Adult and Juvenile Detention | 147 | 154 | 178 | 156 | 94 | 99 | 114 |
| Supai Law Enforcement and Holding Facility | 4 | 1 | 4 | 8 | 50 | 13 | 50 |
| Tohono O'odham Adult Detention Center | 192 | 194 | 199 | 107 | 179 | 181 | 186 |
| Tohono O'odham Juvenile Detention Center | 25 | 25 | 28 | 22 | 114 | 114 | 127 |
| Truxton Canyon Adult Detention Center | 105 | 101 | 105 | 40 | 263 | 253 | 263 |
| Western Navajo Juvenile Corrections Services Center | 12 | 2 | 12 | 36 | 33 | 6 | 33 |
| White Mountain Apache Detention Center | 95 | 81 | 139 | 45 | 211 | 180 | 309 |
| Colorado | | | | | | | |

| State and facility | Inmates in custody[b] | ADP[c] | Peak population in June[d] | Rated capacity[e] | Population on June 30[a] | ADP[a] | Peak population in June[a] |
|---|---|---|---|---|---|---|---|
| Nevada | | | | | | | |
| Eastern Nevada Law Enforcement Adult Detention Facility | 12 | 11 | 20 | 26 | 46% | 42% | 77% |
| New Mexico | | | | | | | |
| Acoma Tribal Police and Holding Facility | 11 | 10 | 11 | 20 | 55% | 50% | 55% |
| Jicarilla Department of Corrections - Adult and Juvenile | 27 | 30 | 45 | 60 | 45 | 50 | 75 |
| Laguna Tribal Police and Detention Center | 52 | 56 | 60 | 43 | 121 | 130 | 140 |
| Navajo Department of Corrections - Crownpoint | 16 | 8 | 17 | 14 | 114 | 57 | 121 |
| Navajo Department of Corrections - Shiprock Police Department and Adult Detention | 52 | 9 | 52 | 34 | 153 | 26 | 153 |
| Navajo Department of Corrections - Tohatchi Youth Detention | 4 | 1 | 6 | 13 | 31 | 8 | 46 |
| Ramah Navajo Police Department and Detention Center | 0 | 1 | 8 | 7 | 0 | 14 | 114 |
| San Juan Pueblo Police Department Holding Facility | 4 | 2 | 6 | 2 | 200 | 100 | 300 |
| Taos Tribal Police Department and Detention | 1 | 1 | 5 | 8 | 13 | 13 | 63 |

## Table 10. (Continued)

| | Number of inmates | | | Percent of capacity[a] | | | |
|---|---|---|---|---|---|---|---|
| State and facility | Inmates in custody[b] | ADP[c] | Peak population in June[d] | Rated capacity[e] | Population on June 30[a] | ADP[a] | Peak population in June[a] |
| Zuni Adult Detention Center | 30 | 25 | 41 | 28 | 107 | 89 | 146 |
| Zuni Juvenile Detention Center | 1 | 2 | 4 | 12 | 8 | 17 | 33 |
| North Dakota | | | | | | | |
| Fort Totten Law Enforcement and Adult Detention Center | 15 | 22 | 42 | 26 | 58% | 85% | 162% |
| Gerald Tex Fox Justice Center Adult Detention | 11 | 13 | 30 | 25 | 44 | 52 | 120 |
| Gerald Tex Fox Justice Center Juvenile Detention | 0 | 1 | 5 | 36 | 0 | 3 | 14 |
| Standing Rock Law Enforcement and Adult Detention Center | 93 | 64 | 86 | 48 | 194% | 133% | 179% |
| Turtle Mountain Law Enforcement Adult Detention | 25 | 25 | 33 | 30 | 83 | 83 | 110 |
| Oklahoma | | | | | | | |
| Iowa Tribal Police Department and Holding Facility | 1 | 0 | 2 | 6 | 17% | 0% | 33% |
| Sac and Fox Juvenile Detention Center | 15 | 24 | 28 | 60 | 25 | 40 | 47 |
| Oregon | | | | | | | |
| Warm Springs Police Department and Adult Detention Center | 40 | 50 | 64 | 51 | 78% | 98% | 125% |
| South Dakota | | | | | | | |

| State and facility | Inmates in custody[b] | ADP[c] | Peak population in June[d] | Rated capacity[e] | Population on June 30[a] | ADP[a] | Peak population in June[a] |
|---|---|---|---|---|---|---|---|
| Cheyenne River Sioux Adult Detention Center | 24 | 24 | 59 | 68 | 35% | 35% | 87% |
| Cheyenne River Sioux Juvenile Detention Center | 7 | 14 | 23 | 10 | 70 | 140 | 230 |
| Ki Yuksa O'Tipi Reintegration Center | 22 | 21 | 35 | 32 | 69 | 66 | 109 |
| Kyle Police Department and Adult Detention | 16 | 18 | 44 | 24 | 67 | 75 | 183 |
| Lower Brule Justice Center - Adult Detention | 33 | 27 | 33 | 38 | 87 | 71 | 87 |
| Lower Brule Justice Center - Juvenile Detention | 0 | 0 | / | 22 | 0 | 0 | 0 |
| Oglala Sioux Tribal Offenders Facility | 95 | 110 | 142 | 144 | 66 | 76 | 99 |
| Rosebud Sioux Tribal Police Department and Adult Detention | 38 | 38 | 77 | 67 | 57 | 57 | 115 |
| Rosebud Sioux Wanbli Wiconi Tipi Juvenile Detention | 22 | 22 | 32 | 47 | 47 | 47 | 68 |
| Sisseton-Wahpeton Law Enforcement Adult Detention Center | 12 | 13 | 21 | 20 | 60 | 65 | 105 |
| Washington | | | | | | | |
| Chehalis Tribal Police Department and Adult Detention Center | 10 | 8 | 12 | 24 | 42% | 33% | 50% |
| Colville Adult Detention Center | 22 | 24 | 28 | 29 | 76 | 83 | 97 |

**Table 10. (Continued)**

| | Number of inmates | | | Percent of capacity[a] | | | |
|---|---|---|---|---|---|---|---|
| State and facility | Inmates in custody[b] | ADP[c] | Peak population in June[d] | Rated capacity[e] | Population on June 30[a] | ADP[a] | Peak population in June[a] |
| Makah Public Safety - Adult Detention | 9 | 7 | 13 | 14 | 64 | 50 | 93 |
| Nisqually Adult Corrections | 73 | 70 | 83 | 70 | 104 | 100 | 119 |
| Puyallup Tribal Law Enforcement and Adult Detention | 2 | 4 | 6 | 10 | 20 | 40 | 60 |
| Quinault Nation Police Department and Holding Facility | 2 | 2 | 4 | 16 | 13 | 13 | 25 |
| Spokane Adult Detention Center | 10 | 9 | 14 | 10 | 100 | 90 | 140 |
| Wisconsin | | | | | | | |
| Menominee Tribal Detention Facility | 53 | 54 | 55 | 45 | 118% | 120% | 122% |
| Wyoming | | | | | | | |
| Wind River Adult Detention Center | 11 | 15 | 29 | 26 | 42% | 58% | 112% |

Note: The total number of inmates for the peak population is not calculated because the most crowded in June varies across the jails. :Not calculated. /Not reported.

[a] Population as a percent of capacity occupied is calculated by dividing the population count of a facility by its rated capacity and multiplying by 100. [b] Adults and juveniles confined in jail facilities on the last weekday in June.

[c] Average daily population (ADP) is the number of inmates confined in June, divided by 30. Detail may not sum to total due to rounding.

[d] Peak population is the population held on the day in June in which the custody population of a facility was the largest..

[e] Rated capacity is the maximum number of beds or inmates assigned by a rating official to a facility. Excludes temporary holding areas.

## Inmates in jails in Indian country, by type of offense, June 2009

| State and facility | Total number of inmates in custody | Number of inmates in custody by type of offense | | | | | | | |
|---|---|---|---|---|---|---|---|---|---|
| | | Domestic violence | Assault | Rape/sexual assault | Other violent | DWI/DUI* | Drug offense | Other | Not reported |
| Total | 2,176 | 252 | 299 | 42 | 168 | 229 | 107 | 955 | 124 |
| Alaska | | | | | | | | | |
| Metlakatla Juvenile Detention Center | 0 | 0 | 0 | 0 | 0 | 0 | 0 | 0 | 0 |
| Metlakatla Police Department and Adult Detention Center | 0 | 0 | 0 | 0 | 0 | 0 | 0 | 0 | 0 |
| Arizona | | | | | | | | | |
| Ak-Chin Tribal Police and Detention Center | 11 | 6 | 3 | 2 | 0 | 0 | 0 | 0 | 0 |
| Colorado River Indian Tribes Adult Detention Center | 37 | 3 | 5 | 3 | 4 | 0 | 0 | 22 | 0 |
| Fort McDowell Police Department and Holding Facility | 8 | 2 | 3 | 1 | 2 | 0 | 0 | 0 | 0 |
| Fort Mohave Tribal Police Department and Holding Facility | 1 | 0 | 1 | 0 | 0 | 0 | 0 | 0 | 0 |
| Gila River Department of Rehabilitation and Supervision | | | | | | | | | |
| - Adult | 149 | 46 | 41 | 0 | 10 | 13 | 4 | 35 | 0 |

**Appendix Table 1. (Continued)**

| State and facility | Total number of inmates in custody | Number of inmates in custody by type of offense | | | | | | | |
|---|---|---|---|---|---|---|---|---|---|
| | | Domestic violence | Assault | Rape/sexual assault | Other violent | DWI/DUI* | Drug offense | Other | Not reported |
| Gila River Department of Rehabilitation and Supervision - | | | | | | | | | |
| Juvenile | 30 | 3 | 8 | 0 | 0 | 0 | 0 | 19 | 0 |
| Navajo Department of Corrections - Chinle | 0 | 0 | 0 | 0 | 0 | 0 | 0 | 0 | 0 |
| Navajo Department of Corrections - Kayenta Police | | | | | | | | | |
| Department and Holiding Facility | 11 | 0 | 0 | 0 | 0 | 0 | 0 | 11 | 0 |
| Navajo Department of Corrections - Tuba City | 17 | 0 | 2 | 0 | 0 | 3 | 1 | 11 | 0 |
| Navajo Department of Corrections - Window Rock | 34 | 2 | 0 | 0 | 13 | 3 | 1 | 15 | 0 |
| Pascua Yaqui Police Department and Holding Facility | 1 | 0 | 0 | 0 | 0 | 0 | 0 | 1 | 0 |
| Salt River Pima-Maricopa Department of Corrections | 25 | 8 | 3 | 2 | 1 | 0 | 0 | 11 | 0 |
| San Carlos Department of Corrections and Rehabilitation - | | | | | | | | | |
| Adult and Juvenile Detention | 147 | 6 | 27 | 1 | 3 | 3 | 18 | 89 | 0 |
| Supai Law Enforcement and Holding Facility | 4 | 0 | 1 | 0 | 0 | 3 | 0 | 0 | 0 |
| Tohono O'odham Adult Detention Center | 192 | 21 | 40 | 7 | 16 | 8 | 5 | 95 | 0 |

| State and facility | Total number of inmates in custody | Number of inmates in custody by type of offense | | | | | | | |
|---|---|---|---|---|---|---|---|---|---|
| | | Domestic violence | Assault | Rape/sexual assault | Other violent | DWI/DUI* | Drug offense | Other | Not reported |
| Tohono O'odham Juvenile Detention Center | 25 | 0 | 4 | 0 | 0 | 0 | 21 | 0 | 0 |
| Truxton Canyon Adult Detention Center | 105 | 34 | 27 | 3 | 21 | 8 | 9 | 3 | 0 |
| Western Navajo Juvenile Corrections Services Center | 12 | 0 | 1 | 0 | 0 | 0 | 0 | 11 | 0 |
| White Mountain Apache Detention Center | 95 | 12 | 22 | 1 | 0 | 2 | 2 | 56 | 0 |
| Colorado | | | | | | | | | |
| Chief Ignacio Justice Center Adult Detention | 34 | 2 | 6 | 0 | 7 | 6 | 5 | 8 | 0 |
| Chief Ignacio Justice Center Juvenile Detention | 10 | 0 | 3 | 0 | 0 | 0 | 0 | 7 | 0 |
| Southern Ute Police Department and Adult Detention | | | | | | | | | |
| Center | 37 | 2 | 4 | 1 | 3 | 4 | 0 | 23 | 0 |
| Idaho Fort Hall Police Department and Adult Detention Center | 9 | 0 | 0 | 0 | 0 | 9 | 0 | 0 | 0 |
| Michigan | | | | | | | | | |
| Saginaw Chippewa Tribal Police Department and Adult | | | | | | | | | |
| Detention Center | 0 | 0 | 0 | 0 | 0 | 0 | 0 | 0 | 0 |

## Appendix Table 1. (Continued)

| State and facility | Total number of inmates in custody | Number of inmates in custody by type of offense | | | | | | | |
|---|---|---|---|---|---|---|---|---|---|
| | | Domestic violence | Assault | Rape/sexual assault | Other violent | DWI/DUI* | Drug offense | Other | Not reported |
| Sault Ste. Marie Tribal Youth Facility | 14 | 0 | 1 | 3 | 0 | 0 | 0 | 10 | 0 |
| Minnesota | | | | | | | | | |
| Red Lake Tribal Justice Center Adult Detention | 36 | 4 | 11 | 1 | 0 | 3 | 1 | 16 | 0 |
| Red Lake Tribal Justice Juvenile Detention | 9 | 0 | 0 | 0 | 0 | 0 | 0 | 9 | 0 |
| Mississippi | | | | | | | | | |
| Choctaw Justice Complex Adult Detention | 38 | 3 | 2 | 0 | 2 | 1 | 3 | 27 | 0 |
| Choctaw Justice Complex Juvenile Detention | 5 | 1 | 0 | 0 | 0 | 0 | 1 | 3 | 0 |
| Montana | | | | | | | | | |
| Blackfeet Adult Detention Center | 31 | 2 | 4 | 0 | 0 | 2 | 1 | 22 | 0 |
| Crow Adult Detention Center | 24 | 2 | 1 | 0 | 6 | 4 | 2 | 9 | 0 |
| Flathead Adult Detention Center | 20 | 3 | 0 | 0 | 0 | 2 | 0 | 15 | 0 |
| Fort Peck Indian Juvenile Services Center | 11 | 0 | 1 | 1 | 1 | 0 | 0 | 8 | 0 |
| Fort Peck Police Department and Adult Detention Center | 31 | 0 | 0 | 0 | 0 | 1 | 0 | 1 | 29 |
| Fort Peck Transitional Living Unit | 2 | 1 | 1 | 0 | 0 | 0 | 0 | 0 | 0 |
| Northern Cheyenne Adult Detention Center | 38 | 3 | 1 | 0 | 0 | 15 | 6 | 13 | 0 |

| | of inmates in custody | Domestic violence | Assault | Rape/sexual assault | Other violent | DWI/DUI* | Drug offense | Other | Not reported |
|---|---|---|---|---|---|---|---|---|---|
| Northern Cheyenne Youth Service Center | 22 | 2 | 4 | 0 | 2 | 1 | 1 | 12 | 0 |
| Rocky Boy Adult Detention Center | 13 | 0 | 2 | 0 | 0 | 1 | 2 | 8 | 0 |
| Nebraska Omaha Tribal Police Department and Adult Detention | 17 | 3 | 2 | 0 | 0 | 3 | 0 | 9 | 0 |
| Nevada | | | | | | | | | |
| Eastern Nevada Law Enforcement Adult Detention Facility | 12 | 1 | 1 | 0 | 1 | 1 | 0 | 8 | 0 |
| New Mexico | | | | | | | | | |
| Acoma Tribal Police and Holding Facility | 11 | 2 | 0 | 1 | 0 | 0 | 0 | 8 | 0 |
| Jicarilla Department of Corrections - Adult and Juvenile | 27 | 0 | 0 | 0 | 0 | 3 | 0 | 24 | 0 |
| Laguna Tribal Police and Detention Center | 52 | 10 | 4 | 6 | 3 | 7 | 0 | 22 | 0 |
| Navajo Department of Corrections - Crownpoint | 16 | 0 | 4 | 0 | 1 | 0 | 0 | 11 | 0 |
| Navajo Department of Corrections - Shiprock Police | | | | | | | | | |
| Department and Adult Detention | 52 | 12 | 6 | 0 | 0 | 9 | 0 | 25 | 0 |
| Navajo Department of Corrections - Tohatchi Youth | | | | | | | | | |
| Detention | 4 | 3 | 0 | 0 | 0 | 0 | 0 | 1 | 0 |

## Appendix Table 1. (Continued)

| State and facility | Total number of inmates in custody | Number of inmates in custody by type of offense | | | | | | | |
|---|---|---|---|---|---|---|---|---|---|
| | | Domestic violence | Assault | Rape/sexual assault | Other violent | DWI/DUI* | Drug offense | Other | Not reported |
| Ramah Navajo Police Department and Detention Center | 0 | 0 | 0 | 0 | 0 | 0 | 0 | 0 | 0 |
| San Juan Pueblo Police Department Holding Facility | 4 | 2 | 0 | 0 | 0 | 2 | 0 | 0 | 0 |
| Taos Tribal Police Department and Detention | 1 | 0 | 0 | 0 | 0 | 0 | 0 | 1 | 0 |
| Zuni Adult Detention Center | 30 | 2 | 3 | 2 | 0 | 5 | 3 | 15 | 0 |
| Zuni Juvenile Detention Center | 1 | 0 | 0 | 0 | 0 | 0 | 0 | 1 | 0 |
| North Dakota | | | | | | | | | |
| Fort Totten Law Enforcement and Adult Detention Center | 15 | 2 | 2 | 0 | 1 | 1 | 1 | 8 | 0 |
| Gerald Tex Fox Justice Center Adult Detention | 11 | 2 | 2 | 1 | 0 | 3 | 2 | 1 | 0 |
| Gerald Tex Fox Justice Center Juvenile Detention | 0 | 0 | 0 | 0 | 0 | 0 | 0 | 0 | 0 |
| Standing Rock Law Enforcement and Adult Detention | | | | | | | | | |
| Center | 93 | 3 | 5 | 0 | 21 | 41 | 0 | 23 | 0 |
| Turtle Mountain Law Enforcement Adult Detention | 25 | 3 | 2 | 0 | 0 | 0 | 0 | 20 | 0 |

|  | of inmates in custody | Domestic violence | Assault | Rape/sexual assault | Other violent | DWI/DUI* | Drug offense | Other | Not reported |
|---|---|---|---|---|---|---|---|---|---|
| Oklahoma |  |  |  |  |  |  |  |  |  |
| Iowa Tribal Police Department and Holding Facility | 1 | 0 | 0 | 0 | 0 | 0 | 0 | 1 | 0 |
| Sac and Fox Juvenile Detention Center | 15 | 0 | 3 | 0 | 0 | 0 | 1 | 11 | 0 |
| Oregon |  |  |  |  |  |  |  |  |  |
| Warm Springs Police Department and Adult Detention Center | 40 | 2 | 8 | 1 | 0 | 6 | 3 | 20 | 0 |
| South Dakota |  |  |  |  |  |  |  |  |  |
| Cheyenne River Sioux Adult Detention Center | 24 | 1 | 1 | 1 | 2 | 2 | 0 | 17 | 0 |
| Cheyenne River Sioux Juvenile Detention Center | 7 | 0 | 1 | 0 | 3 | 0 | 0 | 3 | 0 |
| Ki Yuksa O'Tipi Reintegration Center | 22 | 0 | 3 | 0 | 0 | 0 | 0 | 19 | 0 |
| Kyle Police Department and Adult Detention | 16 | 1 | 0 | 0 | 0 | 0 | 0 | 15 | 0 |
| Lower Brule Justice Center - Adult Detention | 33 | 5 | 2 | 0 | 0 | 20 | 2 | 4 | 0 |
| Lower Brule Justice Center - Juvenile Detention | 0 | 0 | 0 | 0 | 0 | 0 | 0 | 0 | 0 |
| Oglala Sioux Tribal Offenders Facility | 95 | 0 | 0 | 0 | 0 | 0 | 0 | 0 | 95 |
| Rosebud Sioux Tribal Police Department and Adult |  |  |  |  |  |  |  |  |  |

## Appendix Table 1. (Continued)

| State and facility | Total number of inmates in custody | Number of inmates in custody by type of offense | | | | | | | |
|---|---|---|---|---|---|---|---|---|---|
| | | Domestic violence | Assault | Rape/sexual assault | Other violent | DWI/DUI* | Drug offense | Other | Not reported |
| Detention | 38 | 5 | 2 | 0 | 31 | 0 | 0 | 0 | 0 |
| Rosebud Sioux Wanbli Wiconi Tipi Juvenile Detention | 22 | 0 | 4 | 0 | 0 | 1 | 1 | 16 | 0 |
| Sisseton-Wahpeton Law Enforcement Adult Detention | | | | | | | | | |
| Center | 12 | 1 | 0 | 0 | 0 | 5 | 0 | 6 | 0 |
| Washington | | | | | | | | | |
| Chehalis Tribal Police Department and Adult Detention | | | | | | | | | |
| Center | 10 | 0 | 0 | 1 | 0 | 1 | 3 | 5 | 0 |
| Colville Adult Detention Center | 22 | 8 | 5 | 2 | 4 | 2 | 1 | 0 | 0 |
| Makah Public Safety-Adult Detention | 9 | 3 | 0 | 0 | 0 | 0 | 0 | 6 | 0 |
| Nisqually Adult Corrections | 73 | 5 | 0 | 0 | 0 | 13 | 3 | 52 | 0 |
| Puyallup Tribal Law Enforcement and Adult Detention | 2 | 1 | 0 | 0 | 0 | 0 | 0 | 1 | 0 |
| Quinault Nation Police Department and Holding Facility | 2 | 0 | 0 | 1 | 0 | 0 | 0 | 1 | 0 |
| Spokane Adult Detention Center | 10 | 2 | 2 | 0 | 0 | 3 | 0 | 3 | 0 |

| | of inmates in custody | Domestic violence | Assault | Rape/sexual assault | Other violent | DWI/DUI* | Drug offense | Other | Not reported |
|---|---|---|---|---|---|---|---|---|---|
| Wisconsin<br>Menominee Tribal Detention Facility | 53 | 4 | 8 | 0 | 10 | 5 | 4 | 22 | 0 |
| Wyoming<br>Wind River Adult Detention Center | 11 | 1 | 0 | 0 | 0 | 4 | 0 | 6 | 0 |

*Includes driving while intoxicated and driving while under the influence of drugs or alcohol.

# APPENDIX TABLE 2

**Inmates in jails in Indian country, by conviction status, June 2009**

| State and facility | | Conviction status | |
|---|---|---|---|
| | Inmates in custody | Convicted | Unconvicted |
| Total | 2,176 | 1,496 | 680 |
| Alaska | | | |
| Metlakatla Juvenile Detention Center | 0 | 0 | 0 |
| Metlakatla Police Department and Adult Detention Center | 0 | 0 | 0 |
| Arizona | | | |
| Ak-Chin Tribal Police and Detention Center | 11 | 9 | 2 |
| Colorado River Indian Tribes Adult Detention Center | 37 | 32 | 5 |
| Fort McDowell Police Department and Holding Facility | 8 | 6 | 2 |
| Fort Mohave Tribal Police Department and Holding Facility | 1 | 0 | 1 |
| Gila River Department of Rehabilitation and Supervision - Adult | 149 | 93 | 56 |
| Gila River Department of Rehabilitation and Supervision - Juvenile | 30 | 0 | 30 |
| Navajo Department of Correction - Chinle | 0 | 0 | 0 |

## Appendix Table 2. (Continued)

| State and facility | Inmates in custody | Conviction status | |
|---|---|---|---|
| | | Convicted | Unconvicted |
| Navajo Department of Corrections - Kayenta Police Department and Holding | 11 | 0 | 11 |
| Navajo Department of Corrections - Tuba City | 17 | 0 | 17 |
| Navajo Department of Corrections - Window Rock | 34 | 3 | 31 |
| Pascua Yaqui Police Department and Holding Facility | 1 | 0 | 1 |
| Salt River Pima - Maricopa Department of Corrections | 25 | 14 | 11 |
| San Carlos Department of Corrections and Rehabilitation - Adult and Juvenile | 147 | 129 | 18 |
| Supai Law Enforcement and Holding Facility | 4 | 4 | 0 |
| Tohono O'odham Adult Detention Center | 192 | 148 | 44 |
| Tohono O'odham Juvenile Detention Center | 25 | 14 | 11 |
| Truxton Canyon Adult Detention Center | 105 | 103 | 2 |
| Western Navajo Juvenile Corrections Services Center | 12 | 2 | 10 |
| White Mountain Apache Detention Center | 95 | 61 | 34 |
| Colorado | | | |
| Chief Ignacio Justice Center Adult Detention | 34 | 29 | 5 |
| Chief Ignacio Justice Center Juvenile Detention | 10 | 8 | 2 |
| Southern Ute Police Department and Adult Detention Center | 37 | 31 | 6 |
| Idaho | 9 | 9 | 0 |
| Michigan | | | |
| Saginaw Chippewa Tribal Police Department and Adult Detention Center | 0 | 0 | 0 |
| Sault Ste. Marie Tribal Youth Facility | 14 | 13 | 1 |
| Minnesota | | | |
| Red Lake Tribal Justice Center Adult Detention | 36 | 6 | 30 |
| Red Lake Tribal Justice Juvenile Detention | 9 | 5 | 4 |

|  | Inmates in custody | Convicted | Unconvicted |
| --- | --- | --- | --- |
| Mississippi |  |  |  |
| Choctaw Justice Complex Adult Detention | 38 | 28 | 10 |
| Choctaw Justice Complex Juvenile Detention | 5 | 4 | 1 |
| Montana |  |  |  |
| Blackfeet Adult Detention Center | 31 | 20 | 11 |
| Crow Adult Detention Center | 24 | 13 | 11 |
| Flathead Adult Detention Center | 20 | 16 | 4 |
| Fort Peck Indian Juvenile Services Center | 11 | 10 | 1 |
| Fort Peck Police Department and Adult Detention Center | 31 | 25 | 6 |
| Fort Peck Transitional Living Unit | 2 | 2 | 0 |
| Northern Cheyenne Adult Detention Center | 38 | 17 | 21 |
| Northern Cheyenne Youth Service Center | 22 | 8 | 14 |
| Rocky Boy Adult Detention Center | 13 | 13 | 0 |
| Nebraska | 17 | 5 | 12 |
| Nevada | 12 | 9 | 3 |
| New Mexico |  |  |  |
| Acoma Tribal Police and Holding Facility | 11 | 8 | 3 |
| Jicarilla Department of Corrections - Adult and Juvenile | 27 | 26 | 1 |
| Laguna Tribal Police and Detention Center | 52 | 42 | 10 |
| New Mexico (continued) |  |  |  |
| Navajo Department of Corrections - Crownpoint | 16 | 3 | 13 |
| Navajo Department of Corrections - Shiprock Police Department and Adult | 52 | 38 | 14 |
| Navajo Department of Corrections - Tohatchi Youth Detention | 4 | 0 | 4 |
| Ramah Navajo Police Department and Detention Center | 0 | 0 | 0 |

## Appendix Table 2. (Continued)

| State and facility | | Conviction status | |
|---|---|---|---|
| | Inmates in custody | Convicted | Unconvicted |
| San Juan Pueblo Police Department Holding Facility | 4 | 4 | 0 |
| Taos Tribal Police Department and Detention | 1 | 1 | 0 |
| Zuni Adult Detention Center | 30 | 20 | 10 |
| Zuni Juvenile Detention Center | 1 | 0 | 1 |
| North Dakota | | | |
| Fort Totten Law Enforcement and Adult Detention Center | 15 | 9 | 6 |
| Gerald Tex Fox Justice Center Adult Detention | 11 | 2 | 9 |
| Gerald Tex Fox Justice Center Juvenile Detention | 0 | 0 | 0 |
| Standing Rock Law Enforcement and Adult Detention Center | 93 | 87 | 6 |
| Turtle Mountain Law Enforcement Adult Detention | 25 | 22 | 3 |
| Oklahoma | | | |
| Iowa Tribal Police Department and Holding Facility | 1 | 0 | 1 |
| Sac and Fox Juvenile Detention Center | 15 | 6 | 9 |
| Oregon | 40 | 35 | 5 |
| South Dakota | | | |
| Cheyenne River Sioux Adult Detention Center | 24 | 1 | 23 |
| Cheyenne River Sioux Juvenile Detention Center | 7 | 1 | 6 |
| Ki Yuksa O'Tipi Reintegration Center | 22 | 11 | 11 |
| Kyle Police Department and Adult Detention | 16 | 2 | 14 |
| Lower Brule Justice Center - Adult Detention | 33 | 30 | 3 |
| Lower Brule Justice Center - Juvenile Detention | 0 | 0 | 0 |
| Oglala Sioux Tribal Offenders Facility | 95 | 52 | 43 |
| Rosebud Sioux Tribal Police Department and Adult Detention | 38 | 33 | 5 |

|  | Inmates in custody | Convicted | Unconvicted |
| --- | --- | --- | --- |
| Rosebud Sioux Wanbli Wiconi Tipi Juvenile Detention | 22 | 20 | 2 |
| Sisseton-Wahpeton Law Enforcement Adult Detention Center | 12 | 11 | 1 |
| Washington |  |  |  |
| Chehalis Tribal Police Department and Adult Detention Center | 10 | 6 | 4 |
| Colville Adult Detention Center | 22 | 11 | 11 |
| Makah Public Safety - Adult Detention | 9 | 6 | 3 |
| Nisqually Adult Corrections | 73 | 61 | 12 |
| Puyallup Tribal Law Enforcement and Adult Detention | 2 | 1 | 1 |
| Quinault Nation Police Department and Holding Facility | 2 | 2 | 0 |
| Spokane Adult Detention Center | 10 | 8 | 2 |
| Wisconsin<br>Menominee Tribal Detention Facility | 53 | 41 | 12 |
| Wyoming<br>Wind River Adult Detention Center | 11 | 7 | 4 |

# APPENDIX TABLE 3

## Number of adults and juveniles in the custody of jails in Indian country, by sex, June 2009

| State and facility | Adults | | | Juveniles (under age 18) | | |
|---|---|---|---|---|---|---|
| | Total | Male | Female | Total | Male | Female |
| Total | 1,919 | 1,571 | 348 | 257 | 183 | 74 |
| Alaska | | | | | | |
| Metlakatla Juvenile Detention Center | 0 | 0 | 0 | 0 | 0 | 0 |
| Metlakatla Police Department and Adult Detention Center | 0 | 0 | 0 | 0 | 0 | 0 |
| Arizona | | | | | | |
| Ak-Chin Tribal Police and Detention Center | 11 | 10 | 1 | 0 | 0 | 0 |
| Colorado River Indian Tribes Adult Detention Center | 35 | 27 | 8 | 2 | 2 | 0 |
| Fort McDowell Police Department and Holding Facility | 6 | 4 | 2 | 2 | 1 | 1 |
| Fort Mohave Tribal Police Department and Holding Facility | 1 | 1 | 0 | 0 | 0 | 0 |
| Gila River Department of Rehabilitation and Supervision - Adult | 149 | 124 | 25 | 0 | 0 | 0 |
| Gila River Department of Rehabilitation and Supervision - Juvenile | 0 | 0 | 0 | 30 | 20 | 10 |
| Navajo Department of Corrections - Chinle | 0 | 0 | 0 | 0 | 0 | 0 |
| Navajo Department of Corrections - Kayenta Police Department and Holding | | | | | | |

| | Adults | | | Juveniles (under age 18) | | |
|---|---|---|---|---|---|---|
| | Total | Male | Female | Total | Male | Female |
| Facility | 11 | 10 | 1 | 0 | 0 | 0 |
| Navajo Department of Corrections - Tuba City | 17 | 15 | 2 | 0 | 0 | 0 |
| Navajo Department of Corrections - Window Rock | 34 | 30 | 4 | 0 | 0 | 0 |
| Pascua Yaqui Police Department and Holding Facility | 1 | 1 | 0 | 0 | 0 | 0 |
| Salt River Pima-Maricopa Department of Corrections | 22 | 15 | 7 | 3 | 3 | 0 |
| San Carlos Department of Corrections and Rehabilitation - Adult and Juvenile | | | | | | |
| Detention | 125 | 107 | 18 | 22 | 13 | 9 |
| Supai Law Enforcement and Holding Facility | 4 | 3 | 1 | 0 | 0 | 0 |
| Tohono O'odham Adult Detention Center | 192 | 169 | 23 | 0 | 0 | 0 |
| Tohono O'odham Juvenile Detention Center | 0 | 0 | 0 | 25 | 25 | 0 |
| Truxton Canyon Adult Detention Center | 93 | 78 | 15 | 12 | 12 | 0 |
| Western Navajo Juvenile Corrections Services Center | 0 | 0 | 0 | 12 | 9 | 3 |
| White Mountain Apache Detention Center | 95 | 78 | 17 | 0 | 0 | 0 |
| Colorado | | | | | | |
| Chief Ignacio Justice Center Adult Detention | 34 | 26 | 8 | 0 | 0 | 0 |

## Appendix Table 3. (Continued)

| State and facility | Adults | | | Juveniles (under age 18) | | |
|---|---|---|---|---|---|---|
| | Total | Male | Female | Total | Male | Female |
| Chief Ignacio Justice Center Juvenile Detention | 0 | 0 | 0 | 10 | 5 | 5 |
| Southern Ute Police Department and Adult Detention Center | 37 | 30 | 7 | 0 | 0 | 0 |
| Idaho<br>Fort Hall Police Department and Adult Detention Center | 9 | 9 | 0 | 0 | 0 | 0 |
| Michigan | | | | | | |
| Saginaw Chippewa Tribal Police Department and Adult Detention Center | 0 | 0 | 0 | 0 | 0 | 0 |
| Sault Ste. Marie Tribal Youth Facility | 0 | 0 | 0 | 14 | 10 | 4 |
| Minnesota | | | | | | |
| Red Lake Tribal Justice Center Adult Detention | 36 | 30 | 6 | 0 | 0 | 0 |
| Red Lake Tribal Justice Juvenile Detention | 0 | 0 | 0 | 9 | 7 | 2 |
| Mississippi | | | | | | |
| Choctaw Justice Complex Adult Detention | 38 | 35 | 3 | 0 | 0 | 0 |
| Choctaw Justice Complex Juvenile Detention | 0 | 0 | 0 | 5 | 2 | 3 |
| Montana | | | | | | |
| Blackfeet Adult Detention Center | 31 | 22 | 9 | 0 | 0 | 0 |
| Crow Adult Detention Center | 24 | 14 | 10 | 0 | 0 | 0 |

| | Adults | | | Juveniles (under age 18) | | |
|---|---|---|---|---|---|---|
| | Total | Male | Female | Total | Male | Female |
| Flathead Adult Detention Center | 20 | 12 | 8 | 0 | 0 | 0 |
| Fort Peck Indian Juvenile Services Center | 0 | 0 | 0 | 11 | 8 | 3 |
| Fort Peck Police Department and Adult Detention Center | 31 | 22 | 9 | 0 | 0 | 0 |
| Fort Peck Transitional Living Unit | 0 | 0 | 0 | 2 | 2 | 0 |
| Northern Cheyenne Adult Detention Center | 38 | 32 | 6 | 0 | 0 | 0 |
| Northern Cheyenne Youth Service Center | 0 | 0 | 0 | 22 | 10 | 12 |
| Rocky Boy Adult Detention Center | 13 | 9 | 4 | 0 | 0 | 0 |
| Nebraska<br>Omaha Tribal Police Department and Adult Detention | 17 | 14 | 3 | 0 | 0 | 0 |
| Nevada<br>Eastern Nevada Law Enforcement Adult Detention Facility | 12 | 12 | 0 | 0 | 0 | 0 |
| New Mexico | | | | | | |
| Acoma Tribal Police and Holding Facility | 11 | 10 | 1 | 0 | 0 | 0 |
| Jicarilla Department of Corrections - Adult and Juvenile | 24 | 21 | 3 | 3 | 2 | 1 |
| Laguna Tribal Police and Detention Center | 50 | 45 | 5 | 2 | 1 | 1 |
| Navajo Department of Corrections - Crownpoint | 16 | 14 | 2 | 0 | 0 | 0 |
| Navajo Department of Corrections - Shiprock Police Department and Adult | | | | | | |

**Appendix Table 3. (Continued).**

| State and facility | Adults | | | Juveniles (under age 18) | | |
|---|---|---|---|---|---|---|
| | Total | Male | Female | Total | Male | Female |
| Detention | 52 | 48 | 4 | 0 | 0 | 0 |
| Navajo Department of Corrections - Tohatchi Youth Detention | 0 | 0 | 0 | 4 | 3 | 1 |
| Ramah Navajo Police Department and Detention Center | 0 | 0 | 0 | 0 | 0 | 0 |
| San Juan Pueblo Police Department Holding Facility | 4 | 4 | 0 | 0 | 0 | 0 |
| Taos Tribal Police Department and Detention | 1 | 1 | 0 | 0 | 0 | 0 |
| Zuni Adult Detention Center | 30 | 23 | 7 | 0 | 0 | 0 |
| Zuni Juvenile Detention Center | 0 | 0 | 0 | 1 | 0 | 1 |
| North Dakota | | | | | | |
| Fort Totten Law Enforcement and Adult Detention Center | 15 | 12 | 3 | 0 | 0 | 0 |
| Gerald Tex Fox Justice Center Adult Detention | 11 | 9 | 2 | 0 | 0 | 0 |
| Gerald Tex Fox Justice Center Juvenile Detention | 0 | 0 | 0 | 0 | 0 | 0 |
| Standing Rock Law Enforcement and Adult Detention Center | 93 | 68 | 25 | 0 | 0 | 0 |
| Turtle Mountain Law Enforcement Adult Detention | 25 | 21 | 4 | 0 | 0 | 0 |
| Oklahoma | | | | | | |
| Iowa Tribal Police Department and Holding Facility | 1 | 1 | 0 | 0 | 0 | 0 |

| | Adults | | | Juveniles (under age 18) | | |
|---|---|---|---|---|---|---|
| | Total | Male | Female | Total | Male | Female |
| Sac and Fox Juvenile Detention Center | 0 | 0 | 0 | 15 | 14 | 1 |
| Oregon<br>Warm Springs Police Department and Adult Detention Center | 40 | 30 | 10 | 0 | 0 | 0 |
| South Dakota | | | | | | |
| Cheyenne River Sioux Adult Detention Center | 24 | 22 | 2 | 0 | 0 | 0 |
| Cheyenne River Sioux Juvenile Detention Center | 0 | 0 | 0 | 7 | 5 | 2 |
| Ki Yuksa O'Tipi Reintegration Center | 0 | 0 | 0 | 22 | 11 | 11 |
| Kyle Police Department and Adult Detention | 16 | 7 | 9 | 0 | 0 | 0 |
| Lower Brule Justice Center - Adult Detention | 33 | 22 | 11 | 0 | 0 | 0 |
| Lower Brule Justice Center - Juvenile Detention | 0 | 0 | 0 | 0 | 0 | 0 |
| Oglala Sioux Tribal Offenders Facility | 95 | 77 | 18 | 0 | 0 | 0 |
| Rosebud Sioux Tribal Police Department and Adult Detention | 38 | 30 | 8 | 0 | 0 | 0 |
| Rosebud Sioux Wanbli Wiconi Tipi Juvenile Detention | 0 | 0 | 0 | 22 | 18 | 4 |
| Sisseton-Wahpeton Law Enforcement Adult Detention Center | 12 | 9 | 3 | 0 | 0 | 0 |
| Washington | | | | | | |
| Chehalis Tribal Police Department and Adult Detention Center | 10 | 9 | 1 | 0 | 0 | 0 |
| Colville Adult Detention Center | 22 | 20 | 2 | 0 | 0 | 0 |

**Appendix Table 3. (Continued).**

| State and facility | Adults | | | Juveniles (under age 18) | | |
|---|---|---|---|---|---|---|
| | Total | Male | Female | Total | Male | Female |
| Makah Public Safety - Adult Detention | 9 | 7 | 2 | 0 | 0 | 0 |
| Nisqually Adult Corrections | 73 | 58 | 15 | 0 | 0 | 0 |
| Puyallup Tribal Law Enforcement and Adult Detention | 2 | 1 | 1 | 0 | 0 | 0 |
| Quinault Nation Police Department and Holding Facility | 2 | 2 | 0 | 0 | 0 | 0 |
| Spokane Adult Detention Center | 10 | 10 | 0 | 0 | 0 | 0 |
| Wisconsin<br>Menominee Tribal Detention Facility | 53 | 44 | 9 | 0 | 0 | 0 |
| Wyoming<br>Wind River Adult Detention Center | 11 | 7 | 4 | 0 | 0 | 0 |

In: Criminal Justice in Indian Country
Editors: D. Mercato and E. Rojas
ISBN: 978-1-62100-267-3


*Chapter 3*

# UNITED STATES DEPARTMENT OF JUSTICE DECLINATIONS OF INDIAN COUNTRY CRIMINAL MATTERS*

***United States Government Accountability Office***

The Honorable
Byron L. Dorgan
Chairman
Committee on Indian Affairs
United States Senate

The Honorable
John Barrasso
Vice Chairman
Committee on Indian Affairs
United States Senate

The Honorable John Thune
United States Senate

---

* This is an edited, reformatted and augmented version of the United States Government Accountability Office publication, dated on December 13, 2010.

Subject: *U.S. Department of Justice Declinations of Indian Country Criminal Matters*

The Department of Justice (DOJ) has reported that the crime rates experienced by American Indians are two and a half times higher than those experienced by the general population in the United States. Specifically, from 1992 to 2001 American Indians experienced violent crimes at a rate of 101 violent crimes per 1,000 persons annually, compared to the national rate of 41 per 1,000 persons. The federal government plays a major role in prosecuting crimes committed in Indian country. For example, unless a federal statute has granted the state jurisdiction, the federal government has exclusive jurisdiction to prosecute non-Indians who commit crimes against Indians in Indian country, while the federal government and tribal governments both have jurisdiction to prosecute Indian offenders who commit crimes in Indian country. Federal prosecution, however, carries with it the possibility of greater terms of imprisonment, as tribal courts are statutorily limited to a maximum of 3 years imprisonment per offense, regardless of the severity of the offense, for example, a homicide.[1] Because of such jurisdictional and sentencing limitations, tribal communities rely on the federal government to investigate and prosecute a variety of crimes in Indian country.

Members of Congress have raised questions over recent press reports that federal prosecutors have declined to prosecute a significant percentage of Indian country criminal investigations that have been referred to their offices, and you asked us to review this issue. This report addresses the following questions:

1) How many Indian country matters were referred to U.S. Attorneys' offices and what were the declination rates for those matters for fiscal years 2005 through 2009?
2) What are the reasons for the declinations as recorded in the Department of Justice's case management system?

To determine U.S. Attorney declination rates and the reasons for those declinations, we reviewed violent and nonviolent criminal matters from Indian country in DOJ's case management system, the Legal Information Office Network System (LIONS). Specifically, we consolidated records provided for fiscal years 2005 through 2009, the 5 most recent years of data available for violent and nonviolent crimes, into a single data set and analyzed the data to determine declination rates for Indian country matters. However, LIONS does not contain data on all criminal matters in Indian country. Specifically, Indian country matters may be categorized in LIONS as something other than "Indian country," and crimes committed in Indian country that are not referred to a U.S. Attorney's Office (USAO), for instance, crimes over which the state has jurisdiction, are not recorded in LIONS.[2] We interviewed cognizant DOJ officials about the data entry process for new matters, performed electronic testing for obvious errors in accuracy and completeness of the data, and reviewed LIONS documentation to determine that the data in LIONS was sufficiently reliable for the purpose of our review. We also interviewed staff from 4 of the 94 USAOs that had among the largest volumes of Indian country referrals from fiscal years 2005 through 2009. Since we selected a nonprobability sample of USAOs to interview, the information we obtained is not generalizable to all USAOs.[3] However, the interviews provided insights into the factors that may contribute to the difference in declination rates for various types of criminal offenses.

We conducted our work from October 2009 through December 2010 in accordance with all sections of GAO's Quality Assurance Framework that are relevant to our objectives.[4] The framework requires that we plan and perform the engagement to obtain sufficient and appropriate evidence to meet our stated objectives and to discuss any limitations in our work. We believe that the information and data obtained and the analysis conducted provide a reasonable basis for any findings and conclusions in this product. See enclosure I for a more detailed discussion of our scope and methodology.

## Results in Brief

In fiscal years 2005 through 2009, USAOs resolved about 9,000 of the approximately 10,000 Indian country matters referred to their offices by filing for prosecution,[5] declining to prosecute, or administratively closing the matter.[6] USAOs declined to prosecute 50 percent of the 9,000 matters. In addition:

- About 77 percent of the matters received were categorized as violent crimes, and 24 percent as nonviolent crimes.
- Declination rates tended to be higher for violent crimes, which were declined 52 percent of the time, than for nonviolent crimes, which were declined 40 percent of the time. According to staff from the USAOs, the difference in declination rates may be related to the

evidence that is generally available for each type of crime, because, generally, less evidence is available for violent crimes.

- South Dakota and Arizona were the top two districts receiving Indian country matters, with 2,414 and 2,358 matters, respectively.
- The Federal Bureau of Investigation (FBI) and Bureau of Indian Affairs (BIA) were the most prominent referring agencies, with 5,500 and 2,355 matters referred, respectively. Matters referred by the FBI were declined 46 percent of the time by the USAO, and matters from BIA 63 percent of the time. According to USAO, FBI, and BIA officials, this may be attributed to differences in the types of crimes investigated by the two agencies and the agencies' policies on which matters to refer to USAOs.
- Two charge categories accounted for 55 percent of matters referred. There were 2,922 assault matters received (29 percent of the total), while the other leading charge was sexual abuse and related offenses, with 2,594 matters received (26 percent of the total). USAOs declined to prosecute 46 percent of assault matters and 67 percent of sexual abuse and related matters.

The Department of Justice's case management system, LIONS, cited 32 possible reasons associated with declinations of Indian country matters. Three of those reasons were associated with 65 percent of the declinations. They were "weak or insufficient admissible evidence" (42 percent), "no federal offense evident" (18 percent), and "witness problems" (12 percent).[7]

## BACKGROUND

Crimes committed in Indian country may be under the jurisdiction of federal, state, or tribal governments depending on (1) the identity of the offender and victim—that is, Indian or non-Indian, (2) the nature of the alleged crime, (3) the state in which the alleged crime occurred, and (4) whether the crime was committed in Indian country as defined by federal statute.[8] Depending on the specific combination of factors in a given crime, the U.S. Attorneys may have jurisdiction to prosecute crimes committed in Indian country.[9]

The USAO intake process for Indian country criminal matters begins when a law enforcement agency presents an investigation for possible prosecution. Most Indian country crimes are investigated and presented to the

USAO by a tribal law enforcement agency, the FBI, or by criminal investigators from BIA. USAOs refer to all criminal investigations referred to them as "matters," and categorize them as "violent" or "nonviolent" depending on the nature of the alleged crime.[10] DOJ officials noted that receipt of a referral does not mean that a prosecutable case exists at the time the referral is made. Upon further investigation, USAOs may file the matter for prosecution as a case in court or decline to prosecute the matter.[11] When declining to prosecute a criminal matter, USAOs categorize the declination as an immediate declination or a later declination. An immediate declination occurs when the USAO does not open a file on a referral and does not pursue prosecution of the referral. A later declination occurs when the USAO opens a file on the referral, conducts more work on the matter than would be associated with an immediate declination, but ultimately does not pursue prosecution of the referral. Unless otherwise noted, we have combined immediate and later declinations into a single declination category in our analysis. The intake process for Indian country matters referred to USAOs is illustrated in figure 1 below.

Figure 1. Prosecution or Declination Process for Indian Country Matters Referred to a USAO.

## USAOs Declined to Prosecute 50 Percent of the More than 9,000 Matters Received in Fiscal Years 2005 through 2009 that Were Resolved

Approximately 10,000 Indian country matters were referred to USAOs in fiscal years 2005 through 2009, and USAOs declined to prosecute 50 percent of the more than 9,000 matters that were resolved. As of September 30, 2009, about 1,000 of the total matters received were considered pending because a USAO had not yet decided to file for prosecution, decline, or administratively close the matter.[12] Of the matters received, about 77 percent were categorized as violent crimes, and 24 percent as nonviolent crimes. Annual matters received for violent and nonviolent crime, as well as filing and declination information for those matters, are shown in table 1, below.

The overall declination rate for Indian country matters was 50 percent for fiscal years 2005 through 2009, as shown in table 2, below. Note that trends cannot be discerned by comparing individual years because more matters were pending for recent fiscal years than for earlier fiscal years.

**Table 1. Indian Country Matters Received, Fiscal Years 2005 through 2009**

| | Matters received | | | Matters filed for prosecution or declined | | | Not yet filed for prosecution or declined |
|---|---|---|---|---|---|---|---|
| Fiscal year | Violent[a] | Nonviolent[a] | Total received | Filed for prosecution[b] | Immediately declined | Later declined | |
| 2005 | 1,876 | 479 | 2,342 | 977 | 663 | 682 | 20 |
| 2006 | 1,483 | 472 | 1,947 | 858 | 495 | 546 | 48 |
| 2007 | 1,488 | 489 | 1,963 | 1,018 | 331 | 544 | 70 |
| 2008 | 1,491 | 501 | 1,987 | 975 | 323 | 472 | 217 |
| 2009 | 1,342 | 429 | 1,767 | 756 | 201 | 249 | 561 |
| Total | 7,680 | 2,370 | 10,006 | 4,584 | 2,013 | 2,493 | 916 |

Source: GAO analysis of DOJ data.

[a] Some matters are categorized as both violent and nonviolent. Therefore, the sum of the violent and nonviolent categories exceeds the total received.

[b] "Filed for prosecution" includes matters that were not declined, but were closed in LIONS for administrative reasons. These administratively closed matters include, for instance, matters that were combined with another matter for prosecution and were, therefore, not declined.

Overall, declination rates tend to be higher for violent crimes, which were declined 52 percent of the time in fiscal years 2005 through 2009, than for nonviolent crimes, which were declined 40 percent of the time, as shown in tables 3 and 4.

**Table 2. Indian Country Matters Declined, Violent and Nonviolent Crimes, Fiscal Years 2005 through 2009**

| Fiscal year | Matters received | Matters filed for prosecution or declined[a] | Matters declined | Declination rate[b] |
|---|---|---|---|---|
| 2005 | 2,342 | 2,322 | 1,345 | 58% |
| 2006 | 1,947 | 1,899 | 1,041 | 55% |
| 2007 | 1,963 | 1,893 | 875 | 46% |
| 2008 | 1,987 | 1,770 | 795 | 45% |
| 2009 | 1,767 | 1,206 | 450 | 37% |
| Overall | 10,006 | 9,090 | 4,506 | 50% |

[a] "Filed for prosecution" includes matters that were not declined, but were closed in LIONS for administrative reasons. These administratively closed matters include, for instance, matters that were combined with another matter for prosecution and were, therefore, not declined.

[b] Matters received that have not been filed for prosecution, declined, or administratively closed are not included in the declination rate. Trends cannot be discerned by comparing individual years because more matters were pending for recent fiscal years than for earlier fiscal years. As these pending matters are closed, the declination rates may change, particularly for recent fiscal years.

Source: GAO analysis of DOJ data.

**Table 3. Indian Country Matters Declined, Violent Crimes, Fiscal Years 2005 through 2009**

| Fiscal year | Matters received | Matters filed for Prosecution or declined[a] | Matters declined | Declination rate[b] |
|---|---|---|---|---|
| 2005 | 1,876 | 1,864 | 1,095 | 59% |
| 2006 | 1,483 | 1,454 | 805 | 55% |
| 2007 | 1,488 | 1,434 | 732 | 51% |
| 2008 | 1,491 | 1,343 | 669 | 50% |
| 2009 | 1,342 | 898 | 370 | 41% |
| Overall | 7,680 | 6,993 | 3,671 | 52% |

Source: GAO analysis of DOJ data.

[a] "Filed for prosecution" includes matters that were not declined, but were closed in LIONS for administrative reasons. These administratively closed matters include, for instance, matters that were combined with another matter for prosecution and were, therefore, not declined.

[b] Matters received that have not been filed for prosecution, declined, or administratively closed are not included in the declination rate. Trends cannot be discerned by comparing individual years because more matters were pending for recent fiscal years than for earlier fiscal years. As these pending matters are closed, the declination rates may change, particularly for recent fiscal years.

**Table 4. Indian Country Matters Declined, Nonviolent Crimes, Fiscal Years 2005 through 2009**

| Fiscal year | Matters received | Matters filed for prosecution or declined[a] | Matters declined | Declination rate[b] |
|---|---|---|---|---|
| 2005 | 479 | 471 | 256 | 54% |
| 2006 | 472 | 453 | 240 | 53% |
| 2007 | 489 | 473 | 152 | 32% |
| 2008 | 501 | 431 | 126 | 29% |
| 2009 | 429 | 311 | 80 | 26% |
| Overall | 2,370 | 2,139 | 854 | 40% |

Source: GAO analysis of DOJ data.

[a] "Filed for prosecution" includes matters that were not declined, but were closed in LIONS for administrative reasons. These administratively closed matters include, for instance, matters that were combined with another matter for prosecution and were, therefore, not declined.

[b] Matters received that have not been filed for prosecution, declined, or administratively closed are not included in the declination rate. Trends cannot be discerned by comparing individual years because more matters were pending for recent fiscal years than for earlier fiscal years. As these pending matters are closed, the declination rates may change, particularly for recent fiscal years.

According to staff from the USAOs with whom we spoke, the difference in declination rates may reflect the amount and quality of evidence that is often available for each type of crime. Nonviolent crimes, such as the illegal sale of alcohol, tend to have more witnesses, while other nonviolent crimes such as fraud leave more of a "paper trail" than violent crimes. Violent crimes, however, frequently occur outside the presence of witnesses, other than a typically fragile victim—for example, a child or a victim of domestic violence or sexual abuse—and lack documentary evidence. Furthermore, victims of violent crime may not have seen their attacker, may be too frightened to testify against him or her in court, or may have some form of domestic relationship with the suspect causing them to be unwilling to testify in court. The lack of evidence available for violent crimes tends to make them more difficult to prove and, therefore, may result in an increased rate of declination.

### *Five USAO Districts Account for 73 Percent of All Indian Country Criminal Matters Received*

Fifty-one of the 94 USAO districts received Indian country matters from fiscal years 2005 through 2009, although 5 districts account for 73 percent of all Indian country criminal matters received, as shown in figure 2.

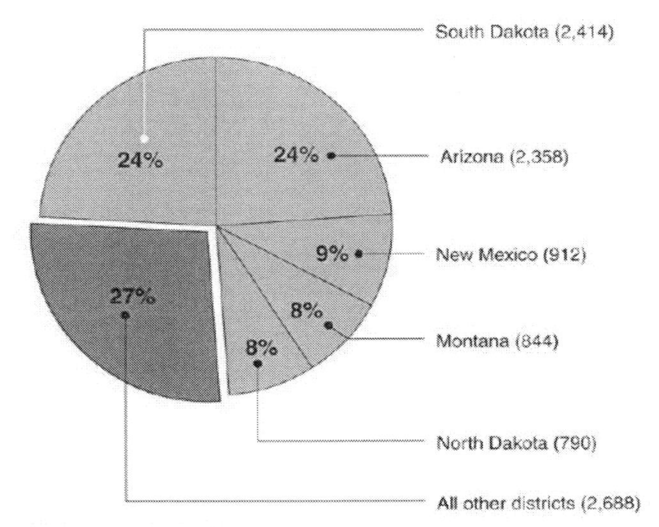


Source: GAO analysis of DOJ data.

Figure 2. Indian Country Matters Received by USAO District, Violent and Nonviolent Crimes, Fiscal Years 2005 through 2009.

After North Dakota, which received 790 Indian country matters from fiscal years 2005 through 2009 and ranked fifth in the number of Indian country criminal matters received, the district with the next largest number of receipts was the Western District of Oklahoma with 301 matters. Twenty-six districts received between 1 and 10 Indian country matters over the period.

For more detail on the number of matters received and declination rates by USAO district, please see enclosure II, tables 7, 8 and 9.

### *Seventy-Nine Percent of Indian Country Matters Were Referred to Usaos by the FBI or BIA*

The FBI and the BIA referred 79 percent of the Indian country matters to the USAOs. The FBI accounted for 55 percent of the total referrals, while the BIA accounted for 24 percent. Tribal law enforcement, the BIA, and the FBI share responsibility for investigating federal offenses in Indian country; however, the LIONS database does not contain a category specifically for referrals from tribal law enforcement authorities. DOJ officials told us that USAOs generally categorize referrals from tribal authorities under the "state/county/municipal authorities" category or the "other" category, and that categorization practices differ between districts. Figure 3, below, shows the number of Indian country matters received by USAOs by referring agency from fiscal years 2005 through 2009.

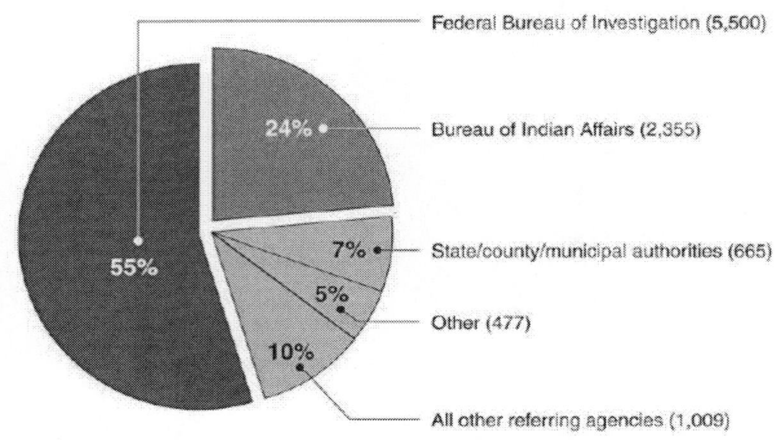


Note: "State/county/municipal authorities" and "Other" categories may include tribal authorities. "Other" is a category in LIONS to track all other agencies that do not have a separate category in the database. "All other referring agencies" combines several smaller LIONS categories in our analysis. Percentages do not add to 100 due to rounding.

Figure 3. Indian Country Matters Received by Referring Agency, Violent and Nonviolent Crimes, Fiscal Years 2005 through 2009.

USAOs declined 63 percent of Indian country criminal matters referred by the BIA and 46 percent of Indian country criminal matters referred by the FBI. Representatives from USAOs, BIA, and FBI told us that this difference in declination rates may be the result of differences in agency protocols for referring matters to a USAO. For example, while FBI officials said that they may elect not to refer matters that they believe lack sufficient evidence for prosecution, BIA officials said that they refer all matters that they investigate to the USAO. Also, one agency may not have a presence in a certain area, leaving the other to make all of the referrals to the USAO. For example, the FBI does not have a presence on some tribal land in Arizona, and so criminal matters from that area are referred by the BIA. Furthermore, FBI officials noted that in many districts USAO guidelines assign primary responsibility for investigation of certain types of crimes to either the FBI or the BIA. For example, the FBI may be primarily responsible for crimes with child victims while the BIA may be responsible for adult rape investigations. These differences in agency protocols for referring matters to a USAO, presence in certain areas of Indian country, and investigative responsibilities may affect the declination rates for the matters referred by the BIA and the FBI.

For more detail on the number of matters received and declination rates by referring agency for violent and nonviolent crimes, see enclosure II, tables 10, 11 and 12.

### *Assault and Sexual Abuse Charges Accounted for 55 Percent of Indian Country Matters Received*

Assault and sexual abuse charges were the leading types of charges in Indian country and accounted for 55 percent of Indian country matters in LIONS, as shown in figure 4 below.

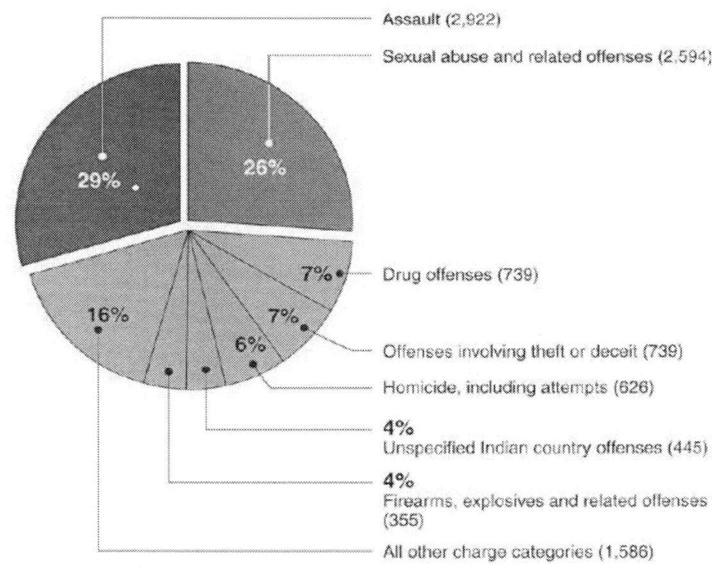


Note: We used the category "Unspecified Indian country offenses" where the LIONS data did not include a specific charged offense but indicated that the alleged criminal conduct took place in Indian country. "All other charge categories" includes specific charges not included in this figure and pending matters where DOJ had not yet decided whether to charge or decline to prosecute. Percentages do not add to 100 due to rounding.

Figure 4. Indian Country Matters Received by Charge, Violent and Nonviolent Crimes, Fiscal Years 2005 through 2009.

Of the two leading Indian country crime charge categories, USAOs declined to prosecute 67 percent of sexual abuse and related matters and declined to prosecute 46 percent of assault matters. USAO officials told us that the difference in declination rates between sexual abuse and assault matters may be the result of the difficulty in obtaining evidence and witnesses in sexual abuse investigations. For example, victims in sexual abuse crimes may not notify law enforcement officials of the crime until long after it occurred, making the collection of nontestimonial, physical evidence difficult or impossible. In addition, sexual assault victims may be unwilling to testify against a perpetrator in court, particularly if they know the perpetrator and are facing pressure not to testify. USAO officials also noted that child victims, in particular, may have difficulty testifying in court against their abuser or experience difficulty in articulating what crimes were committed. In these instances, the matter would likely have to be declined.

For more detail on the number of matters received and declination rates by charge for violent and nonviolent crimes, see enclosure II, tables 13, 14, and 15.

## Reasons for Declinations Varied, but "Weak or Insufficient Evidence" Was the Most Frequently Cited

There were 32 possible declination reasons that could be selected in LIONS and were associated with Indian country criminal matters,[13] and 5 of the reasons were associated with 83 percent of the declinations.[14] "Weak or insufficient admissible evidence" was the reason most frequently associated with declinations, as shown in table 5 below.

DOJ officials have stated that lack of jurisdiction precludes USAO prosecution of certain Indian country crimes. For example, if a non-Indian commits a crime in Indian country and the victim of the crime is also non-Indian, the state rather than the federal government would have jurisdiction to prosecute. However, "Jurisdiction or Venue Problems" was cited in only 2 percent of declinations. At the same time, the selection of reasons for a declination is subject to the prosecutor's discretion and, according to DOJ officials, a prosecutor could choose to use an alternate reason, such as "No Federal Offense Evident," when jurisdiction or venue problems occur. "No Federal Offense Evident" accounted for 18 percent of the declination reasons, as shown in the table above. It is unknown what percentage of these cases may have been declined because the federal government lacked jurisdiction or because the conduct did not meet other elements of the crime.

**Table 5. Frequency of Declination Reasons, Violent and Nonviolent Crimes, Fiscal Years 2005 through 2009**

| Declination reason | Percentage of declinations citing reason[a] |
|---|---|
| Weak or insufficient admissible evidence | 42% |
| No federal offense evident[b] | 18% |
| Witness problems | 12% |
| Lack of evidence of criminal intent | 10% |
| Suspect to be prosecuted by other authorities | 10% |
| All other declination reasons | 26% |

[a] Up to three reasons may be associated with a declination, therefore the sum of percentages exceeds 100.

[b] "No Federal Offense Evident" may include matters declined because of jurisdictional issues.

Source: GAO analysis of DOJ data.

For a list of all of the reasons associated with declinations of Indian country matters, see enclosure II, tables 16, 17, and 18.

We provided a draft of this report to DOJ for review and comment. Their comments are reproduced in enclosure III. DOJ provided additional perspectives on the reasons why USAOs may decline to prosecute a criminal matter, and on their efforts to address public safety challenges in Indian country. DOJ also provided technical comments that we have incorporated where appropriate.

Contact points for our Offices of Congressional Relations and Public Affairs may be found on the last page of this report. Key contributors to this report are listed in enclosure IV.

David C. Maurer
Director, Homeland Security and Justice

Enclosures (4)

# ENCLOSURE I

## Scope and Methodology

To determine U.S. Attorney declination rates and the reasons for those declinations, we reviewed violent and nonviolent criminal matters from Indian country in the Department of Justice's (DOJ) case management system, the Legal Information Office Network System (LIONS). Specifically, we consolidated records provided from fiscal years 2005 through 2009, the 5 most recent years of data available for violent and nonviolent crimes, into a single data set and analyzed the data to determine declination rates for Indian country matters. We considered a matter to be not declined if any one defendant was prosecuted, even if the USAO had declined to prosecute other defendants or had previously declined the matter.

We also interviewed cognizant DOJ officials about the intake and data entry process for Indian country matters, performed electronic testing for obvious errors in accuracy and completeness of the data, and reviewed LIONS documentation to determine that the data we used were sufficiently reliable for the purposes of our review. Nevertheless, certain limitations apply to the Indian country data in LIONS because the system is designed for case management and not primarily for statistical analysis. Specifically, Indian country matters may be categorized in LIONS as something other than "Indian country." For example, a firearms offense involving Indians in Indian country may be categorized only as a firearms matter. Further, crimes committed in Indian country that are not referred to a U.S. Attorney's Office (USAO), for instance, crimes over which the state has jurisdiction, are not recorded in LIONS. Therefore, LIONS does not contain data on all criminal investigations in Indian country. Moreover, the manner in which LIONS is used in individual offices may vary over time in a way that could affect the declination rate, even without changes in Indian country crime frequency or prosecution practices. For example, DOJ officials told us that prior to 2007, the South Dakota USAO opened matters in LIONS to keep information about offenders for possible use if the offenders were later arrested for a prosecutable federal offense. Starting in 2007, the South Dakota USAO changed its LIONS practices and no longer entered those matters in LIONS, which would have the effect of decreasing that office's declination rate.

In addition, we interviewed staff from 4 of the 94 USAOs that had among the largest volumes of Indian country matters from fiscal years 2005 through 2009, the period for which we calculated declination rates. Since we selected a nonprobability sample of USAOs to interview, the information we obtained is not generalizable to all USAOs.[15] However, the interviews provided insights into the factors that may contribute to the difference in declination rates for various types of criminal matters.

We calculated the declination rate for a given fiscal year as the proportion of resolved matters received in that year that were declined at any time during the five year period. A resolved matter is one that the USAO has decided to file for prosecution, decline, or administratively close. For example, we looked at the Indian country matters that USAOs received in fiscal year 2006, and then determined what percentage of the resolved matters were filed for prosecution or administratively closed and what percentage were declined. If a matter was received in fiscal year 2006 and was immediately declined, it was included in the declination rate. Similarly, if a matter was received in fiscal year 2006 and was declined in fiscal year 2008, it was also included in the declination rate for fiscal year 2006 matters. Matters that USAOs had not yet resolved—that is, decided to file for prosecution, decline, or administratively close—were not included in the declination rate.

This approach for calculating declination rates contrasts with an alternate method that has been used by DOJ, in which the number of matters that were received in a given fiscal year is compared with the number of matters declined in that same year. Under this approach, a matter received in 2006 and declined in 2008 would be included in the 2008 declination rate. Furthermore, a matter received in 2008, but which was not filed for prosecution or declined, would also be included in the calculation of the 2008 declination rate. This approach is useful for describing the level of activity related to matters in a given fiscal year, one of the purposes for which DOJ uses the LIONS system, but does not reflect what happened to a matter over time.

In determining the declination rates by charge, we grouped Indian country matters into 19 broad charge categories, listed below in table 6. These categories reflect the lead charge assigned by a prosecutor at intake to indicate the most significant crime alleged.

## Table 6. Charge Categories for Indian Country Criminal Matters

| Charge category | Description of charge category |
|---|---|
| Conservation and environmental offenses | Violations of resource conservation laws contained in Title 16 of the U.S. Code, such as laws protecting National Parks, forests, archeological resources, historic properties, fish, wildlife, and marine mammals; laws protecting public lands (Title 18, Chapter 91); water pollution control laws (Title 33, Chapter 26), and unlawful hunting, trapping, or fishing on Indian land (18 U.S.C. § 1165). |
| Offenses involving theft or deceit | Violations of 17 U.S.C. Chapter 5 (copyright infringement), and 18 U.S.C. Chapter 9 (bankruptcy fraud), Chapter 11 (bribery, graft, and conflicts of interest), Chapter 11a (failure to pay child support), Chapter 25 (counterfeiting and forgery), Chapter 31 (embezzlement and theft), Chapter 42 (extortionate credit transactions), Chapter 47 (fraud and false statements), Chapter 63 (mail and other fraud), Chapter 75 (passport and visa fraud), Chapter 103 (robbery and burglary), Chapter 107 (stowaways), Chapter 113 (stolen property), Chapter 114 (trafficking in tobacco contraband), and 26 U.S.C. Chapter 75 (tax offenses), and certain Indian-related theft offenses, i.e., 18 U.S.C. § 1163 (embezzlement and theft from tribal organizations), 18 U.S.C. § 1167 (theft from gaming establishments in Indian country), and 18 U.S.C. § 1168 (theft by officers or employees of gaming establishments on Indian lands). |
| Obstruction of justice offenses | Violations of 18 U.S.C. § 4 (concealment of a felony), 18 U.S.C. §§ 371-372 (conspiring to commit an offense against the United States or its officers), 18 U.S.C. § 1169 (failure to report child abuse in Indian country), as well as any offenses within the following Chapters of Title 18: Chapter 21 (contempt), Chapter 35 (escape from custody), Chapter 49 (fugitives from justice), Chapter 73 (obstruction of justice), Chapter 75 (perjury), Chapter 207 (release and detention pending judicial proceedings), Chapter 224 (protection of witnesses), Chapter 227 (sentences), and chapter 229 (post-sentence administration). |
| Controlled substance offenses | Violations of the Controlled Substances Act of 1970, which is found in Title 21 of the United States Code, as well as violations of the alcohol prohibitions applicable to Indian country under Title 18, Chapter 53 (18 U.S.C. § 1154-1156). |
| Firearms, explosives, and related offenses | Violations of 18 U.S.C. Chapter 5 (arson), Chapter 40 (explosives), chapter 44 (firearms), and 26 U.S.C. Chapter 53 (certain firearms and destructive devices). |
| Sexual abuse and related offenses | Violations of 18 U.S.C. Chapter 109A (sexual abuse), Chapter 109B (sex offender registration requirements), Chapter 110 (child pornography), and Chapter 117 (involving transportation of the victim forillegal sexual activity). |
| Immigration offenses | Encompasses the general immigration penalty provisions (8 U.S.C. §§ 1324-1330). |
| Property damage or trespass offenses | Violations of 18 U.S.C. Chapter 65 (malicious mischief) and trespass offenses such as 18 U.S.C. § 1793, trespass on Bureau of Prisons land. |
| Gambling offenses | Violations of the following U.S. Code provisions: 15 U.S.C. § 1175, gambling devices prohibited and 18 U.S.C. § 1084, transmission of wagering information. |

**Table 6.**

| Charge category | Description of charge category |
|---|---|
| Racketeering offenses | Violations of 18 U.S.C. chapter 95, including 18 U.S.C. § 1951, interference with commerce by threats or violence; 18 U.S.C. § 1952, interstate and foreign travel or transportation in aid of racketeering enterprises; 18 U.S.C. § 1955, prohibition of illegal gambling businesses; 18 U.S.C. § 1956, laundering of monetary instruments; 18 U.S.C. § 1958, use of interstate commerce facilities in murder-for-hire; and 18 U.S.C. § 1959, violent crimes in aid of racketeering activity. |
| Homicide, including attempts | Violations of 18 U.S.C. chapter 51 (homicide). The offenses within this chapter include murder, manslaughter, and attempted murder or manslaughter, among other things |
| Assault | Violations of 18 U.S.C. Chapter 7. Within this category, assaults may range from simple assault, which is a misdemeanor with a maximum prison exposure of 6 months, to assault with intent to commit murder, which is a felony punishable by up to 20 years imprisonment. |
| Offenses involving threats, force or violence | Violations of 18 U.S.C. Chapter 41 (extortion and threats), Chapter 55 (kidnapping), Chapter 90A (protection of unborn children), and Chapter 110A (domestic violence and stalking). |
| Civil rights offenses | Violations of 18 U.S.C. Chapter 13, which addresses criminal violations of civil rights, such as conspiracy to injure citizens in the exercise of federal rights (18 U.S.C. § 241); willful deprivations of federal rights under color of law (18 U.S.C. § 242); and interference with federally protected activities (18 U.S.C. § 245). |
| Unspecified Indian country offenses | Encompasses LIONS charge values that correspond with the following Indian country provisions: 18 U.S.C. § 1151, which defines the term "Indian country," 18 U.S.C. § 1152, which establishes federal jurisdictionto prosecute a wide variety of crimes in Indian country such as arson, theft, receiving stolen goods, destruction of property, and robbery, provided that either the offender or the victim is an Indian, and 18 U.S.C. § 1153, which establishes federal jurisdiction to prosecute a widevariety of crimes committed by Indians in Indian country, such murder, manslaughter, kidnapping, maiming, incest, felony assault, felony child and a host of sex crimes. Because of the wide array of criminal conduct represented by these charge codes, it is not possible to identify the specific underlying offense, only that the offense charged was committed in Indian country. |
| Juvenile delinquency matters | Encompassed by 18 U.S.C., Chapter 403, which involves violations of federal law committed by persons younger than 18 years old. |
| Postal Service offenses | Violations of law applicable to the Postal Service, which are contained in18 U.S.C. Chapter 83. |
| Pending matters | Matters where DOJ had not yet decided whether to charge or decline to prosecute. |
| Unknown offenses | Encompasses: (1) LIONS charge values for which we were unable to find an associated criminal provision in the U.S. Code; and (2) LIONS charge values that corresponded with a general provision in the U.S. Code such as 18 U.S.C. § 3, accessory after the fact, but did not identifythe underlying offense, such as accessory after the fact to murder. |

Source: GAO.

We conducted our work from October 2009 through December 2010 in accordance with all sections of GAO's Quality Assurance Framework that are relevant to our objectives.[16] The framework requires that we plan and perform the engagement to obtain sufficient and appropriate evidence to meet our stated objectives and to discuss any limitations in our work. We believe that the information and data obtained and the analysis conducted provide a reasonable basis for any findings and conclusions in this product.

# ENCLOSURE II

## Indian Country Matters Received and Declination Rates

Tables 7, 8, and 9, below, show the number of Indian country matters received and declination rates by U.S. Attorney's Office (USAO) district from fiscal years 2005 through 2009. Table 7 includes both violent and nonviolent criminal matters, table 8 shows only violent criminal matters, and table 9 shows only nonviolent criminal matters.

Declination rates are calculated based on the number of matters actually filed for prosecution, declined, or administratively closed by the district office. Declination rates do not include matters that were still "pending," that is, that had not yet been filed for prosecution, declined or administratively closed. We did not calculate declination rates for districts with fewer than 50 matters filed for prosecution, declined or administratively closed from fiscal years 2005 through 2009 because a declination rate would have little meaning when based on such a small number of matters.

**Table 7. Indian Country Matters Received and Declination Rates by USAO District, Violent and Nonviolent Crimes, Fiscal Years 2005 through 2009**

| USAO district | Matters received | Matters filed for prosecution, declined or administratively closed | Matters declined | Declination rate[a] |
|---|---|---|---|---|
| South Dakota | 2,414 | 2,241 | 1,376 | 61% |
| Arizona | 2,358 | 2,178 | 817 | 38% |
| New Mexico | 912 | 746 | 301 | 40% |
| Montana | 844 | 795 | 376 | 47% |
| North Dakota | 790 | 750 | 478 | 64% |

| USAO district | Matters received | Matters filed for prosecution, declined or administratively closed | Matters declined | Declination rate[a] |
|---|---|---|---|---|
| Oklahoma-Western | 301 | 287 | 134 | 47% |
| Wyoming | 225 | 194 | 98 | 51% |
| Idaho | 217 | 200 | 119 | 60% |
| Washington-Eastern | 199 | 183 | 132 | 72% |
| Nebraska | 193 | 171 | 76 | 44% |
| Oregon | 192 | 181 | 122 | 67% |
| Michigan-Western | 164 | 139 | 52 | 37% |
| Nevada | 163 | 151 | 84 | 56% |
| North Carolina-Western | 131 | 125 | 53 | 42% |
| Colorado | 119 | 106 | 38 | 36% |
| Mississippi-Southern | 118 | 88 | 30 | 34% |
| Oklahoma-Eastern | 93 | 66 | 33 | 50% |
| Minnesota | 92 | 77 | 28 | 36% |
| Washington-Western | 85 | 65 | 20 | 31% |
| Utah | 83 | 78 | 22 | 28% |
| Wisconsin-Eastern | 82 | 74 | 16 | 22% |
| Oklahoma-Northern | 78 | 65 | 35 | 54% |
| Alaska | 47 | 42 | 20 | . |
| Michigan-Eastern | 30 | 26 | 19 | . |
| Iowa-Northern | 12 | 12 | 6 | . |
| Alabama-Middle | 5 | 5 | 1 | . |
| Connecticut | 5 | 4 | 3 | . |
| California-Southern | 5 | 4 | 0 | . |
| California-Northern | 4 | 3 | 2 | . |
| New York-Northern | 4 | 3 | 0 | . |
| California-Eastern | 4 | 2 | 2 | . |

**Table 7. (Continued)**

| USAO district | Matters received | Matters filed for prosecution, declined or administratively closed | Matters declined | Declination ratea |
|---|---|---|---|---|
| New York-Western | 4 | 2 | 2 | . |
| Florida Southern | 4 | 2 | 1 | . |
| Louisiana-Western | 3 | 3 | 2 | . |
| Alabama-Southern | 3 | 3 | 1 | . |
| Texas-Southern | 3 | 3 | 0 | . |
| Virginia-Eastern | 3 | 2 | 0 | . |
| Wisconsin-Western | 2 | 2 | 1 | . |
| Maine | 2 | 1 | 1 | . |
| Iowa-Southern | 2 | 1 | 0 | . |
| District of Columbia | 1 | 1 | 1 | . |
| Missouri-Eastern | 1 | 1 | 1 | . |
| Ohio-Southern | 1 | 1 | 1 | . |
| Pennsylvania-Western | 1 | 1 | 1 | . |
| Rhode Island | 1 | 1 | 1 | . |
| Alabama-Northern | 1 | 1 | 0 | . |
| California-Central | 1 | 1 | 0 | . |
| Maryland | 1 | 1 | 0 | . |
| Puerto Rico | 1 | 1 | 0 | . |
| Tennessee-Western | 1 | 1 | 0 | . |
| Pennsylvania-Eastern | 1 | 0 | 0 | . |
| **Overall** | **10,006** | **9,090** | **4,506** | **50%** |

Source: GAO analysis of DOJ data.

[a] Matters received that have not been filed for prosecution, declined, or administratively closed are not included in the declination rate.

**Table 8. Indian Country Matters Received and Declination Rates by USAO District, Violent Crimes, Fiscal Years 2005 through 2009**

| USAO district | Matters received | Matters filed for prosecution, declined or administratively closed | Matters decline | Declination rate[a] |
|---|---|---|---|---|
| South Dakota | 1,808 | 1,689 | 1,094 | 65% |
| Arizona | 1,766 | 1,602 | 746 | 47% |
| New Mexico | 907 | 744 | 300 | 40% |
| North Dakota | 692 | 660 | 410 | 62% |
| Montana | 646 | 622 | 292 | 47% |
| Idaho | 189 | 174 | 100 | 57% |
| Wyoming | 188 | 164 | 79 | 48% |
| Nebraska | 174 | 155 | 69 | 45% |
| Oregon | 166 | 157 | 103 | 66% |
| Washington-Eastern | 161 | 149 | 103 | 69% |
| Oklahoma-Western | 125 | 122 | 77 | 63% |
| North Carolina-Western | 115 | 114 | 46 | 40% |
| Nevada | 115 | 106 | 63 | 59% |
| Michigan-Western | 101 | 82 | 33 | 40% |
| Colorado | 96 | 86 | 30 | 35% |
| Minnesota | 86 | 72 | 26 | 36% |
| Mississippi-Southern | 76 | 59 | 18 | 31% |
| Utah | 73 | 69 | 20 | 29% |
| Wisconsin-Eastern | 63 | 56 | 14 | 25% |
| Washington-Western | 50 | 37 | 7 | . |
| Oklahoma-Northern | 23 | 20 | 12 | . |
| Oklahoma-Eastern | 18 | 16 | 9 | . |
| Michigan-Eastern | 15 | 13 | 10 | . |
| Iowa-Northern | 7 | 7 | 3 | . |
| New York-Northern | 3 | 3 | 0 | . |
| Virginia-Eastern | 3 | 2 | 0 | . |
| Alaska | 2 | 2 | 0 | . |
| California-Eastern | 1 | 1 | 1 | . |
| District of Columbia | 1 | 1 | 1 | . |
| Louisiana-Western | 1 | 1 | 1 | . |

**Table 8. (Continued).**

| USAO district | Matters received | Matters filed for prosecution, declined or administratively closed | Matters decline | Declination rate[a] |
|---|---|---|---|---|
| Missouri-Eastern | 1 | 1 | 1 | . |
| New York-Western | 1 | 1 | 1 | . |
| Pennsylvania-Western | 1 | 1 | 1 | . |
| Rhode Island | 1 | 1 | 1 | . |
| Alabama-Southern | 1 | 1 | 0 | . |
| California-Southern | 1 | 1 | 0 | . |
| Puerto Rico | 1 | 1 | 0 | . |
| Tennessee-Western | 1 | 1 | 0 | . |
| Florida Southern | 1 | 0 | 0 | . |
| Overall | 7,680 | 6,993 | 3,671 | 52% |

Source: GAO analysis of DOJ data.

[a] Matters received that have not been filed for prosecution, declined, or administratively closed are not included in the declination rate.

**Table 9. Indian Country Matters Received and Declination Rates by USAO District, Nonviolent Crimes, Fiscal Years 2005 through 2009**

| USAO district | Matters received | Matters filed for prosecution, declined or administratively closed | Matters declined | Declination rate[a] |
|---|---|---|---|---|
| South Dakota | 619 | 565 | 291 | 52% |
| Arizona | 594 | 578 | 71 | 12% |
| Montana | 199 | 174 | 84 | 48% |
| Oklahoma-Western | 177 | 166 | 57 | 34% |
| North Dakota | 98 | 90 | 68 | 76% |
| Oklahoma-Eastern | 75 | 50 | 24 | 48% |
| Michigan-Western | 65 | 59 | 19 | 32% |
| Oklahoma-Northern | 55 | 45 | 23 | . |
| Nevada | 49 | 46 | 21 | . |
| Alaska | 45 | 40 | 20 | . |
| Wyoming | 45 | 37 | 22 | . |
| Mississippi-Southern | 42 | 29 | 12 | . |
| Washington-Eastern | 38 | 34 | 29 | . |

| USAO district | Matters received | Matters filed for prosecution, declined or administratively closed | Matters declined | Declination ratea |
|---|---|---|---|---|
| Washington-Western | 35 | 28 | 13 | . |
| Idaho | 28 | 26 | 19 | . |
| Oregon | 26 | 24 | 19 | . |
| Colorado | 26 | 23 | 10 | . |
| Wisconsin-Eastern | 19 | 18 | 2 | . |
| Nebraska | 19 | 16 | 7 | . |
| North Carolina-Western | 16 | 11 | 7 | . |
| Minnesota | 15 | 14 | 7 | . |
| Michigan-Eastern | 15 | 13 | 9 | . |
| Utah | 14 | 12 | 2 | . |
| Iowa-Northern | 5 | 5 | 3 | . |
| Alabama-Middle | 5 | 5 | 1 | . |
| Connecticut | 5 | 4 | 3 | . |
| New Mexico | 5 | 2 | 1 | . |
| California-Northern | 4 | 3 | 2 | . |
| California-Southern | 4 | 3 | 0 | . |
| Texas-Southern | 3 | 3 | 0 | . |
| Florida Southern | 3 | 2 | 1 | . |
| California-Eastern | 3 | 1 | 1 | . |
| New York-Western | 3 | 1 | 1 | . |
| Alabama-Southern | 2 | 2 | 1 | . |
| Louisiana-Western | 2 | 2 | 1 | . |
| Wisconsin-Western | 2 | 2 | 1 | . |
| Maine | 2 | 1 | 1 | . |
| Iowa-Southern | 2 | 1 | 0 | . |
| Ohio-Southern | 1 | 1 | 1 | . |
| Alabama-Northern | 1 | 1 | 0 | . |
| California-Central | 1 | 1 | 0 | . |
| Maryland | 1 | 1 | 0 | . |
| New York-Northern | 1 | 0 | 0 | . |
| Pennsylvania-Eastern | 1 | 0 | 0 | . |
| Overall | 2,370 | 2,139 | 854 | 40% |

Source: GAO analysis of DOJ data.

[a] Matters received that have not been filed for prosecution, declined, or administratively closed are not included in the declination rate.

Tables 10, 11, and 12, below, show the number of Indian country matters received and declination rates by referring agency from fiscal years 2005 through 2009. Table 10 includes both violent and nonviolent criminal matters, table 11 shows only violent criminal matters, and table 12 shows only nonviolent criminal matters.

Declination rates are calculated based on the number of matters actually filed for prosecution, declined, or administratively closed by the USAOs. Declination rates do not include matters that were still "pending," that is, that had not yet been filed for prosecution, declined or administratively closed. We did not calculate declination rates for referring agencies with fewer than 50 matters filed for prosecution, declined or administratively closed from fiscal years 2005 through 2009 because a declination rate would have little meaning when based on such a small number of matters.

**Table 10. Indian Country Matters Received and Declination Rates by Referring Agency, Violent and Nonviolent Crimes, Fiscal Years 2005 through 2009**

| Referring agency | Matters received | Matters filed for prosecution, declined or administratively closed | Matters declined | Declination rate[a] |
|---|---|---|---|---|
| Federal Bureau of Investigation | 5,500 | 5,008 | 2,323 | 46% |
| Bureau of Indian Affairs | 2,355 | 2,087 | 1,305 | 63% |
| State/County/Municipal Authorities | 665 | 598 | 303 | 51% |
| Other | 477 | 467 | 387 | 83% |
| Drug Enforcement Administration | 276 | 267 | 10 | 4% |
| Joint State/Local Led Task Force | 119 | 108 | 26 | 24% |
| Bureau of Alcohol, Tobacco, Firearms and Explosives | 103 | 89 | 31 | 35% |
| Immigration and Customs Enforcement | 93 | 92 | 4 | 4% |
| Customs and Border Protection | 60 | 59 | 2 | 3% |

| Referring agency | Matters received | Matters filed for prosecution, declined or administratively closed | Matters declined | Declination rate[a] |
|---|---|---|---|---|
| Other Department of the Interior | 54 | 47 | 27 | . |
| United States Marshals Service | 27 | 25 | 2 | . |
| Other Department of Justice | 19 | 17 | 4 | . |
| Postal Service | 15 | 14 | 4 | . |
| Fish and Wildlife Service | 15 | 13 | 2 | . |
| Office of the Inspector General— Health and Human Services | 14 | 12 | 2 | . |
| Joint Alcohol, Tobacco, Firearms and Explosives/State or Local Task Force | 12 | 12 | 2 | . |
| Joint United States Marshals Service/State or Local Task Force | 11 | 8 | 5 | . |
| National Park Service | 9 | 9 | 3 | . |
| Citizenship and Immigration Services | 7 | 7 | 6 | . |
| Transferred from other USAO | 7 | 7 | 4 | . |
| Indian Health Service/Public Health Service | 7 | 6 | 1 | . |
| United States Secret Service | 7 | 5 | 2 | . |
| Forest Service | 7 | 2 | 2 | . |
| Other Department of Housing and Urban Development | 6 | 5 | 3 | . |
| Office of the Inspector General— Department of Justice | 5 | 3 | 0 | . |
| United States Courts | 4 | 4 | 1 | . |
| Joint Drug Enforcement Administration/State or Local Task Force | 4 | 4 | 0 | . |
| Public Health Service | 3 | 3 | 3 | . |
| Bureau of Land Management | 3 | 3 | 2 | . |

**Table 10. (Continued)**

| Referring agency | Matters received | Matters filed for prosecution, declined or administratively closed | Matters declined | Declination rate[a] |
|---|---|---|---|---|
| Social Security Administration | 3 | 3 | 0 | . |
| Office of the Inspector General—Department of Education | 3 | 1 | 1 | . |
| Air Force | 2 | 2 | 2 | . |
| Navajo and Hopi Indian Relocation | 2 | 2 | 2 | . |
| Other Department of Agriculture | 2 | 2 | 2 | . |
| Department of State | 2 | 2 | 1 | . |
| Office of the Inspector General—Postal Service | 2 | 2 | 0 | . |
| Other Department of Health and Human Services | 2 | 1 | 1 | . |
| Department of Education | 1 | 1 | 1 | . |
| Environmental Protection Agency | 1 | 1 | 1 | . |
| Food and Drug Administration | 1 | 1 | 1 | . |
| Joint Defense/State or Local Task Force | 1 | 1 | 1 | . |
| Metropolitan Police Department—District of Columbia | 1 | 1 | 1 | . |
| Veterans Administration—Utah | 1 | 1 | 1 | . |
| Bureau of Prisons | 1 | 1 | 0 | . |
| Farm Service Agency/Commodity Credit Corp | 1 | 1 | 0 | . |
| Federal Housing Administration | 1 | 1 | 0 | . |
| Internal Revenue Service | 1 | 1 | 0 | . |
| Other Department of Labor | 1 | 1 | 0 | . |
| Parole Commission | 1 | 1 | 0 | . |
| Tennessee Valley Authority Commission | 1 | 1 | 0 | . |
| Veterans Administration—New Mexico/Albuquerque | 1 | 1 | 0 | . |
| National Oceanic and Atmospheric Administration | 1 | 0 | 0 | . |
| Overall | 10,006 | 9,090 | 4,506 | 50% |

Source: GAO analysis of DOJ data.

[a] Matters received that have not been filed for prosecution, declined, or administratively closed are not included in the declination rate.

## Table 11. Indian Country Matters Received and Declination Rates by Referring Agency, Violent Crimes, Fiscal Years 2005 through 2009

| Referring agency | Matters received | Matters filed for prosecution, declined, or administratively closed | Matters declined | Declination rate[a] |
|---|---|---|---|---|
| Federal Bureau of Investigation | 4,779 | 4,377 | 2,029 | 46% |
| Bureau of Indian Affairs | 1,851 | 1,652 | 1,053 | 64% |
| State/County/Municipal Authorities | 558 | 506 | 263 | 52% |
| Other | 311 | 301 | 260 | 86% |
| Bureau of Alcohol, Tobacco, Firearms and Explosives | 56 | 49 | 21 | . |
| Joint Federal Bureau of Investigation/State or Local Task Force | 34 | 27 | 13 | . |
| Other Department of the Interior | 17 | 16 | 11 | . |
| Joint State/Local Led Task Force | 16 | 11 | 4 | . |
| United States Marshals Service | 8 | 7 | 0 | . |
| Other Department of Justice | 6 | 6 | 2 | . |
| Joint Alcohol, Tobacco, Firearms and Explosives/State or Local Task Force | 6 | 6 | 1 | . |
| Transferred from other USAO | 4 | 4 | 3 | . |
| Immigration and Customs Enforcement | 4 | 4 | 0 | . |
| Indian Health Service/Public Health Service | 4 | 3 | 0 | . |
| National Park Service | 3 | 3 | 1 | . |
| Joint United States Marshals Service/State or Local Task Force | 3 | 2 | 1 | . |
| Public Health Service | 2 | 2 | 2 | . |
| Customs and Border Protection | 2 | 2 | 0 | . |
| Joint Drug Enforcement Administration/State or Local Task Force | 2 | 2 | 0 | . |
| United States Secret Service | 2 | 1 | 1 | . |

**Table 11. (Continued).**

| Referring agency | Matters received | Matters filed for prosecution, declined, or administratively closed | Matters declined | Declination rate[a] |
|---|---|---|---|---|
| Air Force | 1 | 1 | 1 | . |
| Joint Defense/State or Local Task Force | 1 | 1 | 1 | . |
| Metropolitan Police Department—District of Columbia | 1 | 1 | 1 | . |
| Navajo and Hopi Indian Relocation | 1 | 1 | 1 | . |
| Postal Service | 1 | 1 | 1 | . |
| Veterans Administration—Utah | 1 | 1 | 1 | . |
| Bureau of Prisons | 1 | 1 | 0 | . |
| Drug Enforcement Administration | 1 | 1 | 0 | . |
| Farm Service Agency/Commodity Credit Corp | 1 | 1 | 0 | . |
| Parole Commission | 1 | 1 | 0 | . |
| United States Courts | 1 | 1 | 0 | . |
| Veterans Administration—New Mexico/Albuquerque | 1 | 1 | 0 | . |
| Overall | 7,680 | 6,993 | 3,671 | 52% |

Source: GAO analysis of DOJ data.

[a] Matters received that have not been filed for prosecution, declined, or administratively closed are not included in the declination rate.

**Table 12. Indian Country Matters Received and Declination Rates by Referring Agency, Nonviolent Crimes, Fiscal Years 2005 through 2009**

| Referring agency | Matters received | Matters filed for prosecution, declined or administratively closed | Matters declined | Declination rate[a] |
|---|---|---|---|---|
| Federal Bureau of Investigation | 749 | 657 | 304 | 46% |
| Bureau of Indian Affairs | 516 | 447 | 261 | 58% |
| Drug Enforcement Administration | 275 | 266 | 10 | 4% |
| Other | 167 | 167 | 127 | 76% |
| State/County/Municipal Authorities | 110 | 95 | 40 | 42% |

| Referring agency | Matters received | Matters filed for prosecution, declined or administratively closed | Matters declined | Declination rate[a] |
|---|---|---|---|---|
| Joint State/Local Led Task Force | 103 | 97 | 22 | 23% |
| Immigration and Customs Enforcement | 89 | 88 | 4 | 5% |
| Customs and Border Protection | 58 | 57 | 2 | 4% |
| Joint Federal Bureau of Investigation/State or Local Task Force | 55 | 53 | 12 | 23% |
| Bureau of Alcohol, Tobacco, Firearms and Explosives | 47 | 40 | 10 | . |
| Other Department of the Interior | 37 | 31 | 16 | . |
| United States Marshals Service | 19 | 18 | 2 | . |
| Fish and Wildlife Service | 15 | 13 | 2 | . |
| Postal Service | 14 | 13 | 3 | . |
| Office of the Inspector General— Health and Human Services | 14 | 12 | 2 | . |
| Other Department of Justice | 13 | 11 | 2 | . |
| Joint United States Marshals Service/State or Local Task Force | 8 | 6 | 4 | . |
| Citizenship and Immigration Services | 7 | 7 | 6 | . |
| Forest Service | 7 | 2 | 2 | . |
| National Park Service | 6 | 6 | 2 | . |
| Joint Alcohol, Tobacco, Firearms and Explosives/State or Local Task Force | 6 | 6 | 1 | . |
| Other Department of Housing and Urban Development | 6 | 5 | 3 | . |
| United States Secret Service | 5 | 4 | 1 | . |
| Office of the Inspector General— Department of Justice | 5 | 3 | 0 | . |
| Bureau of Land Management | 3 | 3 | 2 | . |
| Indian Health Service/Public Health Service | 3 | 3 | 1 | . |

**Table 12. (Continued).**

| Referring agency | Matters received | Matters filed for prosecution, declined or administratively closed | Matters declined | Declination ratea |
|---|---|---|---|---|
| Transferred from other USAO | 3 | 3 | 1 | . |
| United States Courts | 3 | 3 | 1 | . |
| Social Security Administration | 3 | 3 | 0 | . |
| Office of the Inspector General—Department of Education | 3 | 1 | 1 | . |
| Other Department of Agriculture | 2 | 2 | 2 | . |
| Department of State | 2 | 2 | 1 | . |
| Joint Drug Enforcement Administration/State or Local Task Force | 2 | 2 | 0 | . |
| Office of the Inspector General—Postal Service | 2 | 2 | 0 | . |
| Other Department of Health and Human Services | 2 | 1 | 1 | . |
| Air Force | 1 | 1 | 1 | . |
| Department of Education | 1 | 1 | 1 | . |
| Environmental Protection Agency | 1 | 1 | 1 | . |
| Food and Drug Administration | 1 | 1 | 1 | . |
| Navajo and Hopi Indian Relocation | 1 | 1 | 1 | . |
| Public Health Service | 1 | 1 | 1 | . |
| Federal Housing Administration | 1 | 1 | 0 | . |
| Internal Revenue Service | 1 | 1 | 0 | . |
| Other Department of Labor | 1 | 1 | 0 | . |
| Tennessee Valley Authority Commission | 1 | 1 | 0 | . |
| National Oceanic and Atmospheric Administration | 1 | 0 | 0 | . |
| Overall | 2,370 | 2,139 | 854 | 40% |

Source: GAO analysis of DOJ data.

[a] Matters received that have not been filed for prosecution, declined, or administratively closed are not included in the declination rate.

**Table 13. Indian Country Matters Received and Declination Rates by Charge Category, Violent and Nonviolent Crimes, Fiscal Years 2005 through 2009**

| Charge category | Matters received | Matters filed for prosecution, declined or administratively closed | Matters declined | Declination rate[a] |
|---|---|---|---|---|
| Assault | 2,922 | 2,922 | 1,341 | 46% |
| Sexual abuse and related offenses | 2,594 | 2,594 | 1,745 | 67% |
| Pending matters[b] | 990 | 75 | 0 | 0% |
| Drug offenses | 739 | 739 | 136 | 18% |
| Offenses involving theft or deceit | 739 | 738 | 359 | 49% |
| Homicide, including | 626 | 626 | 292 | 47% |
| Unspecified Indian country offenses | 445 | 445 | 297 | 67% |
| Firearms, explosives and related offenses | 355 | 355 | 120 | 34% |
| Unknown | 200 | 200 | 71 | 36% |
| Obstruction of justice offenses | 115 | 115 | 29 | 25% |
| Other offenses involving threats, force or violence | 78 | 78 | 43 | 55% |
| Immigration offenses | 67 | 67 | 3 | 4% |
| Juvenile delinquency matters | 37 | 37 | 15 | . |
| Conservation and environmental offenses | 30 | 30 | 10 | . |
| Civil rights offenses | 25 | 25 | 22 | . |
| Property damage or trespass offenses | 21 | 21 | 12 | . |
| Racketeering offenses | 12 | 12 | 8 | . |
| Postal Service offenses | 9 | 9 | 2 | . |
| Gambling offenses | 2 | 2 | 1 | . |
| Overall | 10,006 | 9,090 | 4,506 | 50% |

Source: GAO analysis of DOJ data.

[a] Matters received that have not been filed for prosecution, declined, or administratively closed are not included in the declination rate.

[b] "Pending matters" includes matters where DOJ had not yet decided whether to charge or decline to prosecute, and 75 matters (reflected in the second data column) that were subsequently filed for prosecution or administratively closed but for which charge information was not available in the data provided by DOJ.

Tables 13, 14, and 15, show the number of Indian country matters received and declination rates by charge category from fiscal years 2005 through 2009. Table 13 includes both violent and nonviolent criminal matters, table 14 shows only violent criminal matters, and table 15 shows only non-violent criminal matters.

Declination rates are calculated based on the number of matters actually filed for prosecution, declined, or administratively closed by the USAOs. Declination rates do not include matters that were still "pending," that is, that had not yet been filed for prosecution, declined or administratively closed. We did not calculate declination rates for charge categories with fewer than 50 matters filed for prosecution, declined or administratively closed from fiscal years 2005 through 2009 because a declination rate would have little meaning when based on such a small number of matters. For a detailed explanation of the specific charges included in each charge category see table 6 in enclosure I.

**Table 14. Indian Country Matters Received and Declination Rates by Charge Category, Violent Crimes, Fiscal Years 2005 through 2009**

| Charge category | Matters received | Matters filed for prosecution, declined or administratively closed | Matters declined | Declination rate[a] |
|---|---|---|---|---|
| Assault | 2,869 | 2,869 | 1,316 | 46% |
| Sexual abuse and related offenses | 2,450 | 2,450 | 1,655 | 68% |
| Pending matters[b] | 752 | 66 | 0 | 0% |
| Homicide, including attempts | 606 | 606 | 280 | 46% |
| Firearms, explosives and related offenses | 266 | 266 | 90 | 34% |
| Unspecified Indian country offenses | 253 | 253 | 130 | 51% |
| Unknown | 131 | 131 | 42 | 32% |
| Offenses involving theft or deceit | 128 | 127 | 51 | 40% |
| Other offenses involving threats, force or violence | 71 | 71 | 38 | 54% |
| Obstruction of justice offenses | 51 | 51 | 15 | 29% |
| Drug offenses | 39 | 39 | 17 | . |
| Juvenile delinquency matters | 28 | 28 | 9 | . |

| Charge category | Matters received | Matters filed for prosecution, declined or administratively closed | Matters declined | Declination rate[a] |
|---|---|---|---|---|
| Civil rights offenses | 21 | 21 | 19 | . |
| Property damage or trespass offenses | 8 | 8 | 5 | . |
| Racketeering offenses | 5 | 5 | 4 | . |
| Immigration offenses | 1 | 1 | 0 | . |
| Postal Service offenses | 1 | 1 | 0 | . |
| Overall | 7,680 | 6,993 | 3,671 | 52% |

Source: GAO analysis of DOJ data.

[a] Matters received that have not been filed for prosecution, declined, or administratively closed are not included in the declination rate.

[b] "Pending matters" includes matters where DOJ had not yet decided whether to charge or decline to prosecute, and 66 matters (reflected in the second data column) that were subsequently filed for prosecution or administratively closed but for which charge information was not available in the data provided by DOJ.

## Table 15. Indian Country Matters Received and Declination Rates by Charge Category, Nonviolent Crimes, Fiscal Years 2005 through 2009

| Charge category | Matters received | Matters filed for prosecution, declined or administratively closed | Matters declined | Declination rate[a] |
|---|---|---|---|---|
| Drug offenses | 700 | 700 | 119 | 17% |
| Offenses involving theft or deceit | 612 | 612 | 309 | 50% |
| Pending matters[b] | 240 | 9 | 0 | . |
| Unspecified Indian country offenses | 193 | 193 | 167 | 87% |
| Sexual abuse and related offenses | 157 | 157 | 96 | 61% |
| Firearms, explosives and related offenses | 90 | 90 | 30 | 33% |
| Assault | 75 | 75 | 35 | 47% |
| Unknown | 71 | 71 | 29 | 41% |
| Immigration offenses | 66 | 66 | 3 | 5% |
| Obstruction of justice offenses | 64 | 64 | 14 | 22% |

**Table 15. (Continued).**

| Charge category | Matters received | Matters filed for prosecution, declined or administratively closed | Matters declined | Declination rate[a] |
|---|---|---|---|---|
| Conservation and environmental offenses | 30 | 30 | 10 | . |
| Homicide, including attempts | 22 | 22 | 14 | . |
| Property damage or trespass offenses | 13 | 13 | 7 | . |
| Juvenile delinquency matters | 9 | 9 | 6 | . |
| Postal Service offenses | 8 | 8 | 2 | . |
| Other offenses involving threats, force or violence | 7 | 7 | 5 | . |
| Racketeering offenses | 7 | 7 | 4 | . |
| Civil rights offenses | 4 | 4 | 3 | . |
| Gambling offenses | 2 | 2 | 1 | . |
| Overall | 2,370 | 2,139 | 854 | 40% |

Source: GAO analysis of DOJ data.

[a] Matters received that have not been filed for prosecution, declined, or administratively closed are not included in the declination rate.

[b] "Pending matters" includes matters where DOJ had not yet decided whether to charge or decline to prosecute, and 9 matters (reflected in the second data column) that were subsequently filed for prosecution or administratively closed but for which charge information was not available in the data provided by DOJ.

Tables 16, 17, and 18, show the reasons provided in LIONS for declinations of Indian country matters. Immediate and later declinations both require one reason to be provided. However, later declinations my also include up to two additional reasons. Therefore, the total number of reasons exceeds the total number of declinations. Table 16 includes reasons provided for both violent and nonviolent criminal matters, table 17 shows only reasons associated with violent criminal matters, and table 18 shows only reasons associated with nonviolent criminal matters.

**Table 16. Frequency of Declination Reasons, Violent and Nonviolent Crimes, Fiscal Years 2005 through 2009**

| Declination reason | Number of declinations citing reason[a] | Percentage of declinationsciting reason[a] |
|---|---|---|
| Weak or insufficient admissible evidence | 1,878 | 42% |
| No federal offense evident | 797 | 18% |
| Witness problems | 537 | 12% |
| Lack of evidence of criminal intent | 467 | 10% |
| Suspect to be prosecuted by other authorities | 457 | 10% |
| Agency request | 161 | 4% |
| Minimal federal interest or no deterrent value | 150 | 3% |
| No known suspect | 117 | 3% |
| Office policy (fails to meet prosecutive guidelines) | 109 | 2% |
| Offender's age, health, prior record, or personal matter | 94 | 2% |
| Jurisdiction or venue problems | 91 | 2% |
| Staleness | 84 | 2% |
| Civil, administrative, or other disciplinary alternative | 80 | 2% |
| Lack of investigative resources | 70 | 2% |
| Juvenile suspect | 65 | 1% |
| Lack of prosecutive resources | 58 | 1% |
| Suspect being prosecuted on other charges | 55 | 1% |
| Suspect deceased | 37 | less than 1% |
| Suspect serving sentence | 25 | less than 1% |
| Statute of limitations | 16 | less than 1% |
| Opened in error/office error | 12 | less than 1% |
| Pretrial diversion completed | 12 | less than 1% |
| Petite policy | 8 | less than 1% |
| Suspect cooperation | 8 | less than 1% |
| Suspect a fugitive | 6 | less than 1% |
| Declined per instructions from DOJ | 5 | less than 1% |
| Local agency referral presented by federal agency | 5 | less than 1% |
| Restitution/arrearage payments made or being made | 4 | less than 1% |
| Department policy | 3 | less than 1% |
| By action of the grand jury (no true bill) | 1 | less than 1% |
| All work completed— to be used for miscellaneous matters | 1 | less than 1% |
| Suspect deported | 1 | less than 1% |

Source: GAO analysis of DOJ data.

[a] Up to three reasons may be associated with a declination. Therefore, the number of reasons cited exceeds the number of declinations for violent and nonviolent crimes of 4,506 and the sum of percentages exceeds 100.

## Table 17. Frequency of Declination Reasons, Violent Crimes, Fiscal Years 2005 through 2009

| Declination reason | Number of declinations citing reason[a] | Percentage of declinationsciting reason[a] |
|---|---|---|
| Weak or insufficient admissible evidence | 1,619 | 44% |
| No federal offense evident | 609 | 17% |
| Witness problems | 505 | 14% |
| Lack of evidence of criminal intent | 374 | 10% |
| Suspect to be prosecuted by other authorities | 354 | 10% |
| Agency request | 121 | 3% |
| No known suspect | 94 | 3% |
| Minimal federal interest or no deterrent value | 91 | 2% |
| Offender's age, health, prior record, or personal matter | 87 | 2% |
| Office policy (fails to meet prosecutive guidelines) | 74 | 2% |
| Jurisdiction or venue problems | 71 | 2% |
| Lack of investigative resources | 62 | 2% |
| Staleness | 58 | 2% |
| Civil, administrative, or other disciplinary alternative | 52 | 1% |
| Juvenile suspect | 52 | 1% |
| Lack of prosecutive resources | 48 | 1% |
| Suspect being prosecuted on other charges | 46 | 1% |
| Suspect deceased | 31 | less than 1% |
| Suspect serving sentence | 21 | less than 1% |
| Statute of limitations | 10 | less than 1% |
| Opened in error/office error | 7 | less than 1% |
| Petite policy | 7 | less than 1% |
| Suspect a fugitive | 6 | less than 1% |
| Declined per instructions from DOJ | 5 | less than 1% |
| Suspect cooperation | 5 | less than 1% |
| Pretrial diversion completed | 4 | less than 1% |
| Local agency referral presented by federal agency | 3 | less than 1% |
| All work completed—to be used for miscellaneous matters | 1 | less than 1% |
| Department policy | 1 | less than 1% |
| Restitution/arrearage payments made or being made | 1 | less than 1% |

Source: GAO analysis of DOJ data.

[a] Up to three reasons may be associated with a declination. Therefore, the number of reasons cited exceeds the number of declinations for violent crimes of 3,671 and the sum of percentages exceeds 100.

**Table 18. Frequency of Declination Reasons, Nonviolent Crimes, Fiscal Years 2005 through 2009**

| Declination reason | Number of declinations citing reason[a] | Percentage of declinationsciting reason[a] |
|---|---|---|
| Weak or insufficient admissible evidence | 266 | 31% |
| No federal offense evident | 190 | 22% |
| Suspect to be prosecuted by other authorities | 104 | 12% |
| Lack of evidence of criminal intent | 94 | 11% |
| Minimal federal interest or no deterrent value | 59 | 7% |
| Agency request | 43 | 5% |
| Office policy (fails to meet prosecutive guidelines) | 35 | 4% |
| Witness problems | 35 | 4% |
| Civil, administrative, or other disciplinary alternative | 28 | 3% |
| Staleness | 27 | 3% |
| No known suspect | 23 | 3% |
| Jurisdiction or venue problems | 20 | 2% |
| Juvenile suspect | 13 | 2% |
| Lack of prosecutive resources | 10 | 1% |
| Suspect being prosecuted on other charges | 9 | 1% |
| Lack of investigative resources | 8 | less than 1% |
| Pretrial diversion completed | 8 | less than 1% |
| Offender's age, health, prior record, or personal matter | 7 | less than 1% |
| Suspect deceased | 7 | less than 1% |
| Statute of limitations | 6 | less than 1% |
| Opened in error/office error | 5 | less than 1% |
| Suspect serving sentence | 4 | less than 1% |
| Restitution/arrearage payments made or being made | 3 | less than 1% |
| Suspect cooperation | 3 | less than 1% |
| Department policy | 2 | less than 1% |
| Local agency referral presented by federal agency | 2 | less than 1% |
| By action of the grand jury (no true bill) | 1 | less than 1% |
| Petite policy | 1 | less than 1% |
| Suspect deported | 1 | less than 1% |

Source: GAO analysis of DOJ data.

[a] Up to three reasons may be associated with a declination. Therefore, the number of reasons cited exceeds the number of declinations for nonviolent crimes of 854 and the sum of percentages exceeds 100.

# ENCLOSURE III

## Comments from the Department of Justice

**U.S. Department of Justice**

*Executive Office for United States Attorneys*
*Office of the Director*

*Main Justice Building, Room 2260* *(202) 252-1000*
*950 Pennsylvania Avenue, N. W.*
*Washington, D.C. 20530*

DEC 0 3 2010

Mr. Glenn Davis
Assistant Director
Government Accountability Office
441 G Street, N.W.
Washington, D.C. 20548

Re: U.S. Department of Justice Declinations of Indian Country Criminal Matters
GAO Engagement Code 440923

Dear Mr. Davis:

Thank you for the opportunity to comment on the report titled "U.S. Department of Justice Declinations of Indian Country Criminal Matters." The Executive Office for United States Attorneys (EOUSA) appreciates GAO's cooperation and efforts on this project. We hope this presentation of declination data will be used constructively to work toward solutions to reducing crime in Indian Country.

We particularly appreciate your team's efforts to present this data in appropriate context. For many of the reasons you have included in your report, the declination data generated by our current Legal Information Office Network System (LIONS) is not an appropriate measure of the dedication and commitment of the United States Attorneys' Offices (USAOs) in Indian Country. As the report recognizes, the receipt of a referral from a law enforcement agency does not mean that a prosecutable case exists. In fact the second most frequent reason given for declinations by the USAOs is "No Federal Offense Evident," i.e., the conduct alleged is not a violation of the Federal statutes setting forth the crimes which can be prosecuted by the United States in Indian Country. Yet another reason cited for declinations is that there is no legal jurisdiction over certain individuals or no legal venue to prosecute the crime in Federal court. In addition, as the report points out, the determination to decline to bring a Federal criminal prosecution does not mean that a crime is left unaddressed. Many cases are declined by the USAOs when the defendant is being prosecuted by other authorities, on other charges, or has been subject to other civil or administrative proceedings or a pretrial diversion program (similar to a period of probation).

The public safety challenges in Indian Country are not uniform. They vary widely from district to district - and from tribe to tribe - based upon unique conditions, a complex set of legal jurisdictional issues, geographic challenges, differences in tribal cultures, and the number of tribes and reservations within a particular district. The officer-to-population ratio still remains lower on Indian reservations than in other jurisdictions across the country, and law enforcement agencies in Indian Country have the unique challenge of patrolling large areas of sparsely populated land. The uniformity of LIONS data and its suitability for statistical analysis are affected by the variances among districts and by the discretion afforded the 93 individual United States Attorneys to use the system to manage their offices to meet local priorities and needs. For example, individual offices may have different criteria for entering matters in LIONS. A change in a LIONS-generated declination rate may be entirely attributable to a change in the office's LIONS policy rather than as a result of any changes in the crime rate or prosecution practices or capabilities in that district. In addition, as the report acknowledges, variations in the practice of law enforcement agencies in referring cases to USAOs can also affect the declination rates of USAOs. As noted, some agencies may refer every allegation, even if unsupported, to a USAO (resulting in a declination), while other agencies may refer only those cases which they believe are fully investigated and ready for prosecution.

More importantly, the data contained in the report must be considered in the context of appropriate prosecutorial decision-making. The decision to charge someone with a crime and to seek to deprive the defendant of his or her liberty represents the exercise of power which must be used judiciously. With respect to all crimes, the United States Attorney's Manual and the Principles of Federal Prosecution provide that Department of Justice attorneys "should initiate or recommend Federal prosecution if he/she believes that the person's conduct constitutes a Federal offense and that the admissible evidence probably will be sufficient to obtain and sustain a conviction. Evidence sufficient to sustain a conviction is required under Rule 29(a), Fed. R. Crim. P., to avoid a judgment of acquittal. Moreover, both as a matter of fundamental fairness and in the interest of the efficient administration of justice, no prosecution should be initiated against any person unless the government believes that the person probably will be found guilty by an unbiased trier of fact." United States Attorneys' Manual Section 9-27.220 (Comment). Each case must be evaluated on the evidence available to the prosecutor. Accordingly, it would not be appropriate to use the data contained in this report to promote any type of prosecutorial quota system or incentives to prosecute a higher number of individuals.

Similarly, the declination rates generated by LIONS data are not an appropriate measure of all the ongoing efforts by United States Attorneys to be actively engaged with their partners in tribal law enforcement. Last year, the Attorney General launched a Department-wide initiative on public safety in tribal communities. A component of that initiative is that every USAO with Indian Country in its district will engage annually in consultation with the tribes in that district, in coordination with the FBI, the Bureau of Indian Affairs, the U.S. Marshals Service, the Drug Enforcement Agency, and the Bureau of Alcohol, Tobacco, Firearms and Explosives, and, where appropriate, state and local law enforcement. In addition USAOs are currently implementing operational plans designed to foster ongoing government-to-government relationships with the tribes; to improve communications with tribal law enforcement regarding charging decisions; to initiate cross-deputization and Special Assistant United States Attorney agreements where appropriate; and to establish training for all relevant criminal justice personnel on issues related to Indian Country criminal jurisdiction and legal issues.

- 3 -

The public safety challenges confronting Indian Country are great, and the Department's enhanced efforts in Indian Country can be resource intensive. We are pleased that the FY 2011 President's Budget requests $448.8 million in total resources for initiatives in Indian Country. New investments include significant grant resources for addressing a broad range of criminal justice issues and additional FBI agents to help tribal communities combat illegal drug use, trafficking, and violent crime.

The Department has a responsibility to build a successful and sustainable response to the scourge of violent crime on reservations. In partnership with tribes, our goal is to find and implement solutions to immediate and long-term public safety challenges confronting Indian Country. Thank you for your time and attention to this important matter.

Sincerely,

H. Marshall Jarrett
Director

## End Notes

[1] The Tribal Law and Order Act of 2010 (Pub. L. No. 111-211, tit. II, 124 Stat. 2258, 2261 (2010)) provides tribes with authority to sentence certain convicted Indian offenders for up to 3 years of imprisonment, provided that they afford additional pretrial and trial protections to safeguard the rights of the accused. See 25 U.S.C. § 1302. Before the passage of the act on July 29, 2010 the sentencing authority of tribes was limited to one year.

[2] For example, states have jurisdiction over crimes occurring in Indian country where both parties are non-Indians. In addition, the federal government has enacted statutes giving certain states authority to prosecute crimes committed by or against Indians in Indian country. See, e.g., 18 U.S.C. § 1162, which confers such jurisdiction for all, or parts, of Indian country in Alaska, California, Minnesota, Nebraska, Oregon, and Wisconsin.

[3] Results from nonprobability samples cannot be used to make inferences about a population, because in a nonprobability sample some elements of the population being studied have no chance or an unknown chance of being selected as part of the sample.

[4] This is the first of two efforts related to tribal justice issues that we reviewed in response to your request during this time. The second effort is focused on the challenges that select tribes face in adjudicating Indian country crimes, and collaboration between the Department of the Interior and DOJ to support tribal justice systems. We expect to issue the final results from that effort in 2011.

[5] As of September 30, 2009, about 1,000 of the 10,000 matters were pending action by the USAOs.

[6] Administratively closed matters were not declined, but were closed in LIONS for administrative reasons. These include, for instance, matters that were combined with another matter for prosecution and were, therefore, not declined.

[7] Up to three reasons may be associated with a declination; therefore, the sum of the individual percentages for the three reasons presented here exceeds 65.

[8] The term "Indian country" refers to all land within the limits of any Indian reservation under the jurisdiction of the U.S. government, all dependent Indian communities within U.S. borders,

and all existing Indian allotments, including any rights-of-way running through an allotment. See 18 U.S.C. § 1151.

[9] The tribal government also has jurisdiction to prosecute Indian offenders who commit crimes in Indian country, even in circumstances where federal jurisdiction exists.

[10] There are no fixed criteria for USAOs in categorizing violent versus nonviolent matters. DOJ officials told us that the categorization is made at the discretion of the prosecutor depending on the nature of the alleged crime and that categorization practices may differ among districts.

[11] In the event USAO declines to prosecute a matter, it must coordinate with appropriate tribal justice officials regarding the use of evidence relevant to the prosecution of the case in a tribal court with concurrent jurisdiction, that is, declined cases involving Indian offenders. See 25 U.S.C. § 2809(a)(3).

[12] We calculated the declination rate as the number of matters declined divided by the number of matters that were resolved—that is, filed for prosecution, declined, or administratively closed. We did not include pending matters given that action had not yet been taken on them. See enclosure I for a more detailed discussion of our methodology.

[13] LIONS tracks only the declination reasons chosen by the USAOs and not case-specific facts behind individual declinations.

[14] Up to three reasons may be associated with a declination; therefore, the sum of percentages for the top five reasons exceeds 83.

[15] Results from nonprobability samples cannot be used to make inferences about a population, because in a nonprobability sample some elements of the population being studied have no chance or an unknown chance of being selected as part of the sample.

[16] This is the first of two efforts related to tribal justice issues that we reviewed in response to your request during this time. The second effort is focused on the challenges that select tribes face in adjudicating Indian country crimes, and collaboration between the Department of the Interior and DOJ to support tribal justice systems. We expect to issue the final results from that effort in 2011.

# INDEX

D



E



F



G



H

## R



## S



## T



## U



## V



## W